Chic & Unique
CELEBRATION
Cakes

30 FRESH DESIGNS TO BRIGHTEN SPECIAL OCCASIONS

Chic & Unique
CELEBRATION
Cakes

ZOE CLARK

David and Charles
www.bakeme.com

A DAVID & CHARLES BOOK
© F&W Media International, LTD 2011

David & Charles is an imprint of F&W Media International, LTD
Brunel House, Forde Close, Newton Abbot, TQ12 4PU, UK

F&W Media International, LTD is a subsidiary of F+W Media Inc.
4700 East Galbraith Road, Cincinnati, OH 45236, USA

First published in the UK and USA in 2011

A catalogue record for this book is available from the
British Library.

ISBN-13: 978-0-7153-3838-4 paperback
ISBN-10: 0-7153-3838-2 paperback

Printed in China by RR Donnelley
for F&W Media International, LTD
Brunel House, Forde Close, Newton Abbot, TQ12 4PU, UK

Publisher Alison Myer
Acquisitions Editor Jennifer Fox-Proverbs
Desk Editor Jeni Hennah
Project Editor Beth Dymond
Proofreader Jo Richardson
Art Editors Kevin Mansfield and Sarah Underhill
Photographer Sian Irvine
Senior Production Controller Kelly Smith

F+W Media Inc. publishes high-quality books on a wide
range of subjects. For more great book ideas visit:
www.bakeme.com

Contents

INTRODUCTION

This, my third book, features a collection of stylish and elegant cake designs, all different from one other but each in my simple signature feminine style.

The main focus of the designs featured in this book is on colour and tone, which has a great significance in decorating and styling cakes. From stark monochrome black and white creations and bright Arabian shades to soft pastel tones and sparkling icy styles, my aim is to emphasize the importance of colour in making a simple design extremely effective, transforming it to tie in with any occasion.

The book has ten chapters, each featuring one main tiered cake and two smaller complementary designs, such as cupcakes, fondant fancies or cookies, which can be made individually or in addition to the main cake project. Most of the cakes are shaped around three or four tiers. These can easily be scaled down to a smaller design, such as a double or single tier. I have given each chapter a central theme, whether it is snowflakes for your Christmas party, a beautiful bridal cent or a simple colour scheme that will be pe for any spec celebration.

Although I have included clear instructions on how to reproduce each of the designs exactly, please feel free to unleash your creativity. Adapt the designs and experiment with colour and shape to make your cake individual. You will find handy tips on how to do this in each of the stages to give your cakes that personal touch.

I have chosen these designs specifically to suit a wide range of skill levels. With simple-to-follow step-by-step instructions and hints on easier, no-fuss variations, each section includes a variety of techniques such as stencil work and handcrafted flowers designed to help you to develop and perfect your skills.

Whether you're a first time baker or a qualified professional, this book is intended to inspire and enhance your imagination, and hopefully to encourage you to create your very own designs. I hope you have as much fun and pleasure making the cakes and cookies as I did designing and creating them.

Enjoy!

TOOLS AND EQUIPMENT

The following basic tools are essential for baking the cakes in this book.
It is important to have all your tools and equipment to hand before you start baking.

Baking essentials

✤ **Large electric mixer** for making cakes, buttercream and royal icing

✤ **Kitchen scales** for weighing out ingredients

✤ **Measuring spoons** for measuring small quantities

✤ **Mixing bowls** for mixing ingredients

✤ **Spatulas** for mixing and gently folding together cake mixes

✤ **Cake tins** for baking cakes

✤ **Tartlet tins and/or muffin trays** for baking cupcakes

✤ **Baking trays** for baking cookies

✤ **Wire racks** for cooling cakes and icing fondant fancies

GENERAL EQUIPMENT

✤ **Greaseproof (wax) paper or baking parchment** for lining tins and to use under icing during preparation

✤ **Clingfilm (plastic wrap)** for covering icing to prevent drying out and for wrapping cookie dough

✤ **Large non-stick board** for rolling out icing on

✤ **Non-slip mat** to put under the board so that it doesn't slip on the work surface

✤ **Large and small non-stick rolling pins** for rolling out icing and marzipan

✤ **Large and small sharp knife** for cutting and shaping icing

✤ **Large serrated knife** for carving and sculpting cakes

✤ **Cake leveller** for cutting even, level layers of sponge

✤ **Cake card** is a special card, thinner than a cake board, to which you can attach miniature cakes

✤ **Large and small palette knife** for applying buttercream and ganache

✤ **Icing or marzipan spacers** to give a guide to the thickness of icing and marzipan when rolling out

✤ **Icing smoothers** for smoothing icing

✤ **Spirit level** for checking that cakes are level when stacking them

✤ **Metal ruler** for measuring different heights and lengths

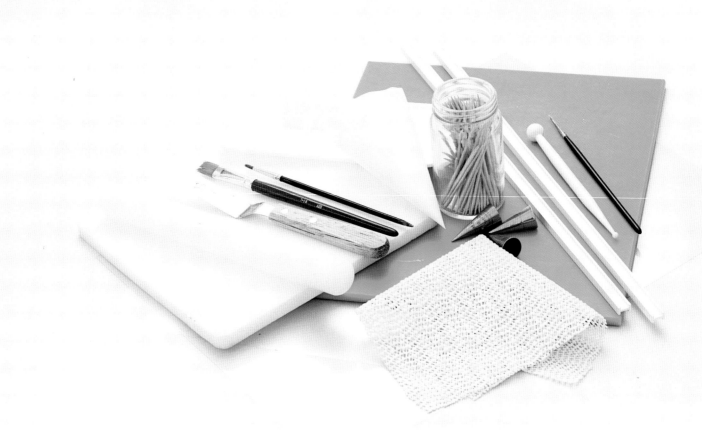

Creative tools

- ❖ **Hollow plastic dowels** for assembling cakes

- ❖ **Turntable** for layering cakes

- ❖ **Double-sided tape** to attach ribbon around cakes, boards and pillars

- ❖ **Piping (pastry) bags** for royal icing decorations

- ❖ **Piping tubes (tips)** for piping royal icing

- ❖ **Cocktail sticks (toothpicks) or cel sticks** for colouring and curling icing

- ❖ **Acetate or cellophane sheets** for run-out icing decorations, or for covering icing if you are interrupted while working to keep it from drying out

- ❖ **Edible glue** for sticking icing to icing

- ❖ **Edible pens** for marking positioning guides

- ❖ **Needle scriber** for lightly scoring positioning guides and bursting bubbles in icing

- ❖ **Cake-top marking template** for finding/marking the centre of cakes and marking where dowels should be placed

- ❖ **Pastry brush** for brushing sugar syrup and apricot masking spread or strained jam (jelly) onto cakes

- ❖ **Fine paintbrushes** for gluing and painting

- ❖ **Dusting brushes** for brushing edible dust onto icing

- ❖ **Dipping fork** for dipping fondant fancies in fondant icing

- ❖ **Ball tool** for frilling or thinning the edge of flower paste

- ❖ **Foam pad** for softening and frilling flower paste

- ❖ **Frill cutters** for cutting borders and pretty edges

- ❖ **Blossom and star plunger cutters** for cutting blossoms and stars

- ❖ **Circle cutters** for cutting circles of various sizes

- ❖ **Shaped cutters** for cutting out shapes such as leaves, diamonds, stars and wedding cakes

- ❖ **Five-petal rose cutters** for making large blossoms (see Chandelier Chic)

- ❖ **Moulds** such as lace moulds (see Bows and Blossoms)

MAGNIFICENT MONOCHROME

Think of a chandelier and it immediately conjures up an image
of luxury and glamour, of spacious rooms and high ceilings,
of ballrooms, mansions and sophisticated five-star hotels.

Here I have taken the classic theme of the chandelier design and
used simple stencilling to reverse its traditional silver, gold or crystal
colour scheme into a black and silver design that looks striking
against the crisp white icing. This chic monochrome effect
highlights the delicate shape and symmetry of the chandelier
with its sweeping chains, bold candles and elegant pear drops.

"*A chandelier instantly brings a touch of elegance, class and, of course, light to any room*"

Chandelier chic

This eye-catching cake design is made using chandelier stencils, which, after a little practice, are extremely easy to work with. The extra depth of the tiers allows space to exhibit the chandeliers at different levels and the beautiful flowers soften the angular shape of the cake. Painting the grey stencil work with silver lustre dust gives a touch of sparkle, creating a glamorous effect.

MATERIALS

❖ One 10cm (4in) wide x 10cm (4in) deep square cake, one 15cm (6in) wide x 12cm (4½in) deep square cake and one 23cm (9in) wide x 13cm (5in) deep square cake (see Baking and Covering Techniques)

❖ One 35cm (14in) square white iced cake board (see Icing Cake Boards)

❖ One quantity of royal icing

❖ 100g (3½oz) white flower paste

❖ Black food colouring

❖ Edible lustre dust: silver, white satin

❖ Clear alcohol

❖ Edible glue

EQUIPMENT

❖ Eight hollow dowels, approximately 30cm (12in) long (see Assembling Tiered Cakes)

❖ Chandelier stencils (Designer Stencils)*

❖ Large five-petal rose cutter (FMM)

❖ Large 6cm (2½in) single rose petal cutter

❖ 15mm (5/8in) white double-faced satin ribbon

❖ Black cord trim (optional)

❖ Small palette knife or side scraper

❖ Damp cloth

❖ Small piping (pastry) bag and no. 1 piping tube (tip)

❖ Fine paintbrush

❖ Foam pad and ball tool

❖ Paint palette or sphere-shaped mould

❖ Dusting brush

❖ Double-sided tape

* When ordering, you will need to make a special request for a smaller version of the stencil to be made for the smaller 7.5cm (3in) chandelier.

1 Bake, prepare and ice your cakes in white sugarpaste at least 12–24 hours in advance (see Baking and Covering Techniques). Start by dowelling the bottom and middle tiers of the cake (see Assembling Tiered Cakes). Stick the base cake onto the 35cm (14in) square cake board and assemble the other tiers on top using white royal icing to secure them in place. Wrap satin ribbon around the base of each tier and secure in place with double-sided tape.

2 Mix black food colouring into some royal icing until you have a very dark charcoal grey colour. The icing will darken to black as it dries.

3 Position the larger stencil against the side of the cake and gently hold it in place. Use a small palette knife or side scraper to smear a thin coating of the black royal icing over the stencil. Ensure that the entire design is covered and scrape away any excess icing with one hand while the other hand is holding the stencil. Return any excess icing to the bowl and cover it with a damp cloth to prevent it from drying out. Carefully and fairly swiftly, peel away the stencil from the cake to reveal the chandelier design.

4 Repeat this process using the larger and smaller stencils and both colours until you have stencilled designs all over the cake. If you overlap any stencils, make sure the bottom one is completely dry first. This can be tricky, so only overlap them if necessary. For the lower hanging chandeliers, you will need to hold the stencil lower down and pipe small dots, using a no. 1 piping tube (tip) (see Piping with Royal Icing), from the top of the chandelier to the top of the cake tier to make a chain.

TIP

Be careful not to move the stencil or you will not achieve a clean result.

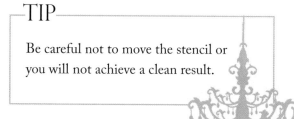

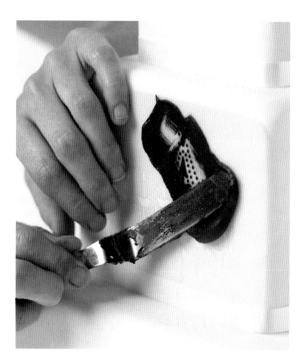

5 Paint the grey chandeliers with silver lustre dust mixed with clear alcohol to make a liquid paste.

6 To make the flowers, start by rolling two large marble-sized balls using white flower paste. Thinly roll out some more white flower paste and cut out four large flowers using the five-petal rose cutter. Use the points on the petals of the cutter to make indentations on each petal of the flowers.

TIP

For extra sparkle, paint some edible glue around the candles and dab on edible glitter with a fine paintbrush.

7 Soften the edges of the flowers on a foam pad using the ball tool. Take one flower and wrap the petals around the prepared ball-shaped centre, overlapping them as you go. Attach the petals in place using some edible glue. Take another cut-out flower and cup this around the inner petals to form the second layer. Use the remaining cut-out shapes to make a second flower, then sit them in a paint palette or small sphere-shaped mould to dry for an hour or so.

8 For the outer petals, cut out ten individual petals with the large rose petal cutter from thinly rolled-out flower paste. Soften the edges of the petals as before and press them into the paint palette or sphere mould to shape them slightly. Set them aside to dry a little. When they are still semi-wet, attach the point of each petal on the underside of the flower in the centre, overlapping them as before like a rose.

9 Dust the flowers with white satin lustre dust and attach to the ledges of the cake with royal icing. Finish by securing satin ribbon around the cake board with double-sided tape, which you can top with black cord trim, if you like.

Elegant mini cakes

These gorgeous mini cakes are beautifully decorated with drop-line piping to echo the elegant patterns and chains of the chandelier. The simple black lines stand out strikingly against the white icing and the crisp white floral decoration gives the cakes a touch of glamour.

Mark the centre point on each side of the cake, then mark two points on either side of the central point slightly in from the corner. Colour some of the royal icing black, then fill a small piping (pastry) bag with a no. 1 piping tube (tip) and use this to pipe lines between the points, allowing them to drop down slightly in the centre. Pipe two teardrops into the points, then pipe dots down the cake for the chains. The last dot at the bottom of each line is slightly bigger than the rest. Pipe two more teardrops halfway down the centre row. The flower is made in the same way as for the large flowers on the main cake but using the medium five-petal cutter rather than the individual cutters to form the outer petals.

YOU'LL ALSO NEED

✤ 5cm (2in) square mini cakes (see Miniature Cakes)

✤ Small and medium size five-petal rose cutters (FMM)

Stunning stencil cookies

These stylish matching cookies are so simple to create and are decorated using the same techniques and stencils as the main project. They are perfect for adding a touch of class to any glitzy occasion.

Outline and flood the cookies with white royal icing (see Royal-iced Cookies). Allow 4–8 hours for the icing to dry, then use the stencil to paint on the chandelier design as for the main project. The grey chandeliers can be painted with lustre dust as before. Finish by piping a dotted border around the edge of the cookies using black or grey royal icing and a no. 1 tube (tip). Paint the grey dots with silver lustre dust.

YOU'LL ALSO NEED
❖ 7.5cm (3in) square cookies

AUTUMN LEAVES

What better way to honour an autumn celebration than with these handsome chocolate pieces? These rustic creations really capture the wonderful crisp colours and mellow fruitfulness of nature at this time of year. By focusing on the climbing branches, plump berries and golden leaves, they instantly evoke a classic autumn scene.

Chocolate is a great medium to work with for this theme and will appeal to the chocoholics in your life. The different shades of chocolate brown give a striking autumnal impression, which would be perfect for a seasonal wedding, a retirement party or to celebrate an autumn birthday.

*"Using chocolate
really adds to the rustic
appeal of this striking
autumnal piece"*

Climbing branches

This beautiful tiered cake has been covered in chocolate-flavoured sugarpaste but you could use milk chocolate paste instead, which makes it a great option for anyone who doesn't like the sweet taste of icing. I have enhanced the leaves by brushing on metallic lustre dusts to give them a gorgeous shine.

MATERIALS

- One 10cm (4in), one 15cm (6in), one 20cm (8in) and one 25cm (10in) cake, each 10cm (4in) deep, prepared and iced in mid-brown sugarpaste (mixed equal parts of chocolate-flavoured icing and ivory) or milk chocolate paste (see Baking and Covering Techniques)

- Two 30cm (12in) square thick cake boards, stuck together, then covered with chocolate-flavoured icing (see Icing Cake Boards)

- 100g (3½oz) mid-brown sugarpaste (mixed equal parts of chocolate-flavoured icing and ivory or milk chocolate paste)

- 150g (5½oz) dark chocolate modelling paste

- 50g (1¾oz) milk chocolate modelling paste

- 50g (1¾oz) neutral marzipan

- Half quantity of royal icing

- Red food colouring

- Metallic edible lustre dusts: bronze, gold, copper

- Red edible dust

- CMC (optional)

- Edible glue

EQUIPMENT

- 12 hollow pieces of dowels cut to size (see Assembling Tiered Cakes)

- Leaf cutter and mould

- 15mm (5/8in) double-faced dark brown satin ribbon

- Icing smoothers

- Small sharp knife

- Dresden tool

- Dusting brushes

- Bumpy foam or crinkled foil

- Fine paintbrush

- Double-sided tape

1 Dowel and assemble the cake (see Assembling Tiered Cakes).

2 Use the mid-brown sugarpaste or milk chocolate paste to evenly roll out a long sausage shape and carefully wrap around the base of each tier. Start by using your hands, then use an icing smoother as the sausage gets thinner. For the larger tier you might need more than one piece to cover the circumference of the cake. Join the pieces as neatly as possible by trimming the joins with a sharp knife.

3 Knead the dark chocolate modelling paste until it becomes soft and pliable and roll out some more sausage shapes of different lengths so that they come to a point gradually at one end. Mark indentations along the pieces using a Dresden tool.

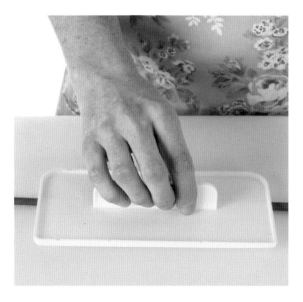

4 Brush a very small amount of edible glue onto the cake where the branch is to be positioned and carefully stick it in place. Start with the larger branches and work your way up the cake, attaching the smaller and shorter branches as you go to look like part of a tree.

5 To make the leaves, thinly roll out some dark chocolate modelling paste and cut out the shapes using the leaf cutter. Brush the veiner with some lustre dust and press the leaves into the mould.

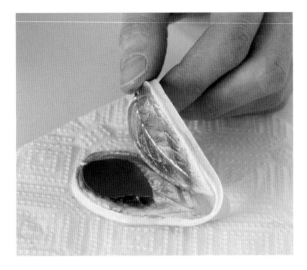

6 Shape the points of the leaves so that they take on a natural shape and place them on some bumpy foam or crinkled foil to dry and stiffen a little.

7 Brush the leaves with the different metallic lustre dusts to give them an autumnal glow. Repeat this with an equal amount of milk chocolate modelling paste mixed into the dark chocolate modelling paste to make some lighter-coloured leaves.

8 Stick the leaves onto the cake using edible glue. Allow some of the leaves to rise up from the tops of the tiers and off the sides of the cake.

9 To make the berries, colour some marzipan with a little red food colouring and roll small marbled-sized pieces into balls.

10 Shade the berries with red edible dust or the metallic shades of edible lustre dust. Attach them to the branches tucked under the leaves using a small amount of edible glue or brown royal icing. Finish by securing the dark brown satin ribbon around the cake board with double-sided tape.

Leaf-topped fancies

Fondant fancies are a lovely alternative to cupcakes and are really fashionable at the moment. They are much lighter and more delicate than an iced mini cake, and their square shape really complements the square tiers of the larger design.

Pipe branches onto the fancies with some brown-coloured royal icing before attaching the dusted leaves and berries, made in the same way as for the main project.

YOU'LL ALSO NEED
* Freshly dipped dark brown fondant fancies (see Fondant Fancies)
* Brown cupcake cases (liners)

Tempting truffles

These luxurious truffles are so easy to make and taste divine. They are a simple way of transforming any of your leftover chocolate sponge cake into a mouth-watering treat.

Break up the chocolate sponge cake completely and moisten it with a small amount of ganache, warmed to melt (ensure that it is not too hot or it will split), until the mixture all comes together. Roll marble-sized balls and place them back in the refrigerator or freezer. Melt some chocolate and put on some disposable gloves, then one at a time dip the chocolate balls into the melted chocolate. Roll them around in your hand until they are lightly coated all over and place them on some greaseproof (wax) paper to set. Roll them in cocoa powder (unsweetened cocoa) before serving.

> **YOU'LL ALSO NEED**
> - Chocolate sponge cake (trimmings are fine)
> - Ganache
> - Chocolate callets
> - Cocoa powder (unsweetened cocoa)
> - Greaseproof (wax) paper

PERIDOT PEONIES

The beautiful white peony flowers and fresh August greens featured here perfectly set the tone for a warm outdoor wedding or summer celebration. These delicate blooms look stunning when accentuated by the darker green leaves, which provide a gentle contrast to the softer background.

To embellish these designs, I have used brush embroidery; one of my favourite methods for decorating cakes and cookies. By simply drawing an outline with royal icing and using a damp brush to pull the icing inwards, you can quickly achieve an interesting finish and texture on the smooth icing.

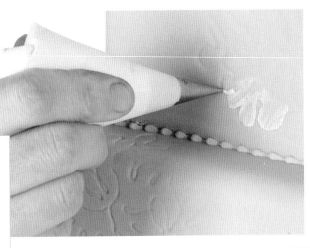

"*I used an actual swatch of lace from a beautiful bridal gown to perfectly recreate its stylish floral design*"

Lacy lovely

Brides often like their wedding cake to reflect the design of their dress and here I have imprinted an actual swatch of lace taken from a bridal gown. To make an impression in the cake, simply press your piece of lace onto the icing using a smoother. If you can't find any suitable lace, you can use a floral embosser instead or scribe your design onto the cake. To recreate my peony design you can use the templates provided. After brush embroidering over the imprinted peonies, try over-piping around the outlines of the flowers to help them to stand proud from the cake.

MATERIALS

✤ One 10cm (4in), one 15cm (6in), one 20cm (8in) and one 28cm (11in) square peridot green iced cake, each 10cm (4in) deep, iced no more than four hours in advance (see Baking and Covering Techniques)

✤ One 35cm (14in) square cake board covered with pale green sugarpaste (see Icing Cake Boards)

✤ One quantity of royal icing

✤ 100g (3½oz) white flower paste

✤ 100g (3½oz) pale green flower paste

✤ Paste food colourings: spruce/moss green, ivory

✤ Edible dusts: yellow, green, aubergine

✤ Edible glue

EQUIPMENT

✤ 12 hollow pieces of dowels cut to size (see Assembling Tiered Cakes)

✤ Peony-shaped pieces of lace (or use the floral and leaf templates with a needle scriber – see Templates)

✤ 26- and 24-gauge wire

✤ Peony petal and leaf cutters and veiner

✤ Approximately 70 hammerhead stamens (half a bunch)

✤ Flower pick

✤ 15mm (5/8in) ivory double-faced satin ribbon

✤ Icing smoothers

✤ Small piping (pastry) bags and piping tubes (tips): nos. 1 and 1.5

✤ No. 2 size fine paintbrush

✤ Small pliers or strong scissors

✤ Green florist tape

✤ Dusting brushes

✤ Small grooved board

✤ Veining tool

✤ Apple tray

✤ Double-sided tape

TIP

If you are imprinting into the cake, the sugarpaste needs to be fairly soft. If you are scribing onto the cake, the cakes need to be covered at least 24 hours in advance.

1 Dowel and assemble the four tiers onto the 35cm (14in) cake board (see Assembling Tiered Cakes). Colour some more royal icing the same colour as the cake and pipe a 'snail trail' border around the base of each tier (see Piping with Royal Icing).

2 Mark the pattern onto the cake, starting with the flowers. Hold the lace against the side of the cake and using the smoother fairly firmly, press the material into the sugarpaste, being careful not to move the lace as you are doing so. Space the flowers over the cake randomly but evenly. Press the leaf designs around the flowers in the same way.

3 Colour some royal icing ivory and fill a small piping (pastry) bag with a no. 1.5 piping tube (tip). Pipe around the outline of the flowers and, using a damp fine paintbrush, drag the icing inwards towards the centre of the flower. Complete up to half of each flower at a time, otherwise the outline will dry out before you get the chance to do the brushwork. If there are any thin areas, go over them again with some more royal icing. Repeat for the leaves using green-coloured royal icing.

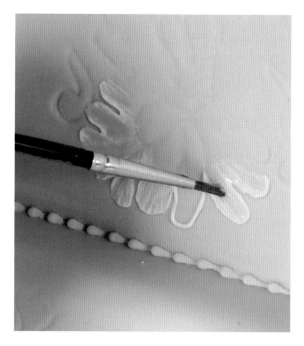

4 Insert a no. 1 tube (tip) into another piping (pastry) bag and fill it with some more ivory royal icing. Pipe around the outlines of the flowers.

5 For the peony, make three small teardrops from pale green flower paste. Cut three 12cm (4¾in) pieces of 26-gauge wire, hook and moisten the ends with edible glue, then insert into each teardrop. Pinch one side of each teardrop to make a ridge and curl the tip over to the ridged side. Tape the teardrops together using florist tape, stretching it as you go to make it stick. Dust the stamens with yellow edible dust and tape them around the pistil.

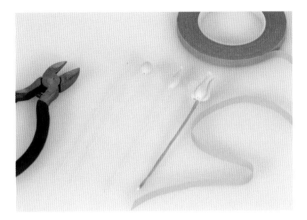

6 To make the petals, roll out white flower paste on the grooved board, leaving a thick ridge in the centre for the wire. Cut out a petal with the medium cutter and insert a 12cm (4¾in) piece of 26-gauge edible glue-moistened wire into the base. Press the petal into the veiner, return it to the board and run the veining tool back and forth across the top edge to make it frilly. Set aside to dry in an apple tray. Make six medium and eight or nine larger petals.

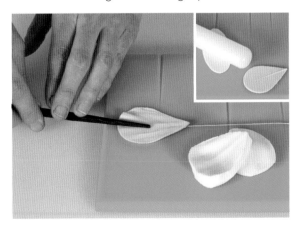

7 Tape the six smaller petals around the stamen and add six of the larger petals in between them. The remaining petals can be taped on where required to add volume to the flowers. Set aside.

8 Add additional green colouring to the pale green flower paste and roll it out as before, leaving a ridge for the wire. Cut out the leaves with the cutters – at least two or three sets of three (each set is made up of one three-point and two two-point shapes). Insert some 24-gauge wire at least halfway into the base and dust them with green and aubergine dust. Tape the set of three leaves together before taping them onto the peony stem. Cut the stem to approximately 7cm (2¾in) and insert into a flower pick.

9 Finish by assembling the peony on top of the cake and attach the ivory satin ribbon around the base board with double-sided tape.

Irresistible ivory cake

Experiment with different colours to suit your colour scheme.
The look of this ivory cake is quite different to the main design,
but ties in beautifully with the subtle colour changes of the
larger cake and would be perfect for a traditional wedding. Here
I have used the scriber to imprint the pattern onto the cake.

Trace the floral and leaf templates onto some greaseproof (wax) paper. Pin
the templates onto the cake and scribe over the design. Pipe and brush the
royal icing as for the main project, but make the flowers a pale green colour
to stand out against the ivory cake.

YOU'LL ALSO NEED

* 15cm (6in) square cake 10cm
  (4in) deep, iced in ivory at
  least 24 hours in advance (see
  Baking and Covering
  Techniques)
* 23cm (9in) square cake board,
  iced in pale green (see Icing
  Cake Boards)
* Floral and leaf templates (see
  Templates)
* Greaseproof (wax) paper
* Pins
* Needle scriber

Fabulously floral cookies

These adorable wedding cake cookies are the perfect accompaniment to your bridal theme. Display them in pretty bags embellished with ribbons so that your guests can take a little piece of your summer wedding away with them.

Roll out the sugarpaste and cut out the wedding cakes. Stick the sugarpaste onto the cookies with boiled apricot jam (do this 24 hours in advance if you are scribing onto the cookies). Imprint the floral design onto the cake and use the brush embroidery technique from the main design for decoration.

SWEET SUNSHINE

My most treasured items of clothing are embellished with broderie anglaise trims. I absolutely adore the delicate, repetitive patterns made from the little holes and embroidered stitching, which create a pure and simple design reminiscent of sweet baby bonnets and pretty English petticoats. In this chapter I have tried to recreate this idea in sugar.

Traditionally, broderie anglaise is a white lace material but you can experiment with different colour schemes to suit the occasion. Here the sweet pastel yellow colour scheme brings a glimmer of sunshine to the designs, which would be perfect for a christening or a Mother's Day celebration.

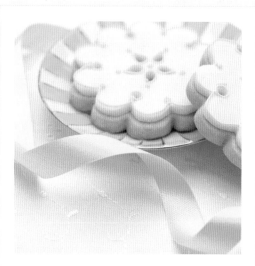 

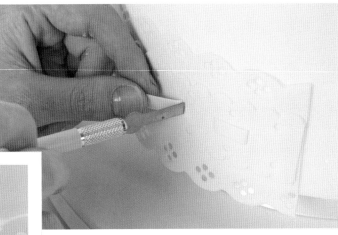

"*Broderie anglaise beautifully incorporates features of embroidery, cutwork and needle lace that arose in England in the 19th century*"

Embroidered eyelets

Create this charming design by cutting out tiny holes from thinly rolled-out strips of icing cut with scallop-edged strip cutters. The beauty and intricacy of the design comes from the addition of the ribbon threaded through the lacy strips, cleverly made by attaching rectangular pieces of yellow flower paste at intervals around the centre of the strip, then creating a beautiful bow centrepiece to really impress your guests. The final piping decoration adds a delicate decorative touch, typical of the broderie anglaise style.

MATERIALS

❖ One 25cm (5in) round cake, one 18cm (7in) round cake and one 23cm (9in) round cake, each 9cm (3½in) deep, prepared and iced in white at least 12–24 hours in advance (see Baking and Decorating Techniques)

❖ One 33cm (13in) round cake board, covered with white sugarpaste (see Icing Cake Boards)

❖ Two 10cm (4in) round cake boards or one 10cm (4in) round, 2.5cm (1in) deep spacer dummy

❖ Two 15cm (6in) round cake boards/drums

❖ Two 20cm (8in) round cake boards

❖ 400g (14oz) pale yellow flower paste

❖ 50g (1¾oz) white flower paste

❖ Half quantity of royal icing

❖ Yellow food colouring

❖ Edible glue

EQUIPMENT

❖ 6 hollow pieces of dowels cut to size (see Assembling Tiered Cakes)

❖ Endless garret frill cutter (Orchard Products)

❖ Ribbon insertion tool

❖ Cardboard template: 6 x 15mm (¼ x 5/8in)

❖ Butterfly cookie cutter

❖ Eyelet cutters

❖ 2.5cm (1in) white satin ribbon

❖ 15mm (5/8in) white double-faced satin ribbon

❖ Large and small sharp knives

❖ Small piping (pastry) bags and piping tubes (tips): nos. 1, 1.5 and 4

❖ Waxed paper and concertina-folded card to fit the butterfly

❖ Double-sided tape

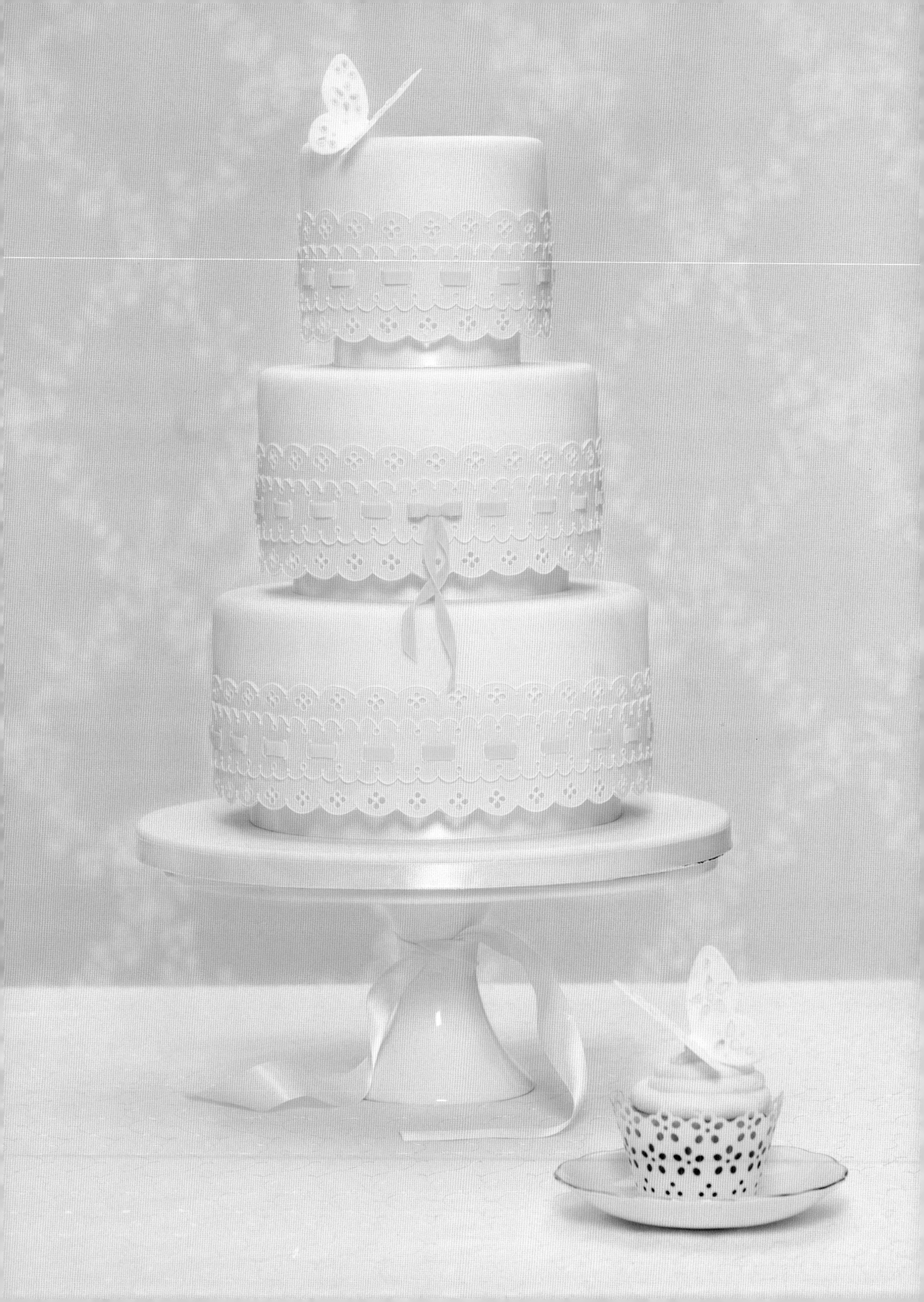

1 Stick the two 10cm (4in) boards together with royal icing. Repeat with the two 15cm (6in) and 20cm (8in) boards. Dowel the bottom 23cm (9in) and middle 18cm (7in) tiers (see Assembling Tiered Cakes).

2 Stick the 20cm (8in) boards onto the centre of the base board with royal icing and wrap the 2.5cm (1in) white ribbon around them, securing it in place with double-sided tape. Smear some more royal icing on the 20cm (8in) boards and stack the 23cm (9in) cake on top. Repeat for the middle and top tiers until the cake is completely assembled.

3 Roll out a long strip of yellow flower paste at least 10cm (4in) wide and approximately 30cm (12in) long. Using the wider frill of the garret frill cutter, cut a scalloped edge either side of the strip parallel to each other. Use the no. 4 piping tube (tip) to cut four holes in a diamond shape in each cove along the length of the icing. Stick the strips around the cakes with edible glue so that the bottom edge hangs below the bottom of the cakes. You will need to cut enough strips to go around each tier.

4 Roll out some more strips of flower paste approximately 5cm (2in) wide and cut a scalloped edge as before, but this time using the narrow frill cutter. Using the no. 4 piping tube (tip), cut holes at alternate points along the flower paste on both sides. Stick the cut pieces onto the cake in the centre of the wider strips.

5 Using the ribbon insertion tool and a rectangular template, mark 6 x 15mm (¼ x 5/8in) slits 15mm (5/8in) apart around the centre of the yellow trim.

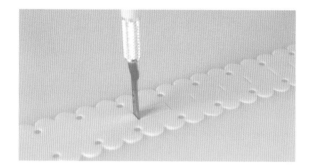

6 Colour the remaining flower paste with some more yellow food paste until you have a stronger colour. Thinly roll the icing out and cut out 5mm (3/16in) wide strips. From these strips, cut 18mm (¾in) lengths to form the ribbon to wrap around each tier. Using the ribbon insertion tool and some edible glue, attach the tiny rectangular pieces of ribbon to the cake at each end. The centre of each piece should not touch the cake and should be slightly curved to give the impression that it is being threaded in and out.

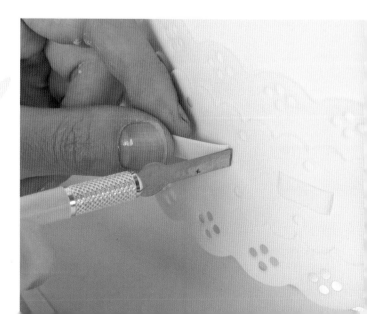

7 Make a small bow from more 5mm (3/16in) wide strips of flower paste for the middle tier. Form the loops from a 10cm (4in) long strip, with both ends turned in and pinched in the centre. For the knot, wrap a 2cm (¾in) strip around the centre and join at the back with edible glue. The bow simply replaces a section where the inserted ribbon would be placed. Use approximately 15cm (6in) long strips for the tails and stick them onto the cake before the bow. Twist them around slightly to fall in a delicate fashion.

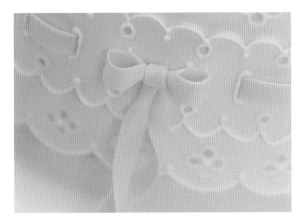

8 Place a no. 1 tube (tip) inside a small piping (pastry) bag and fill it with soft-peak white royal icing. Carefully pipe around the outline of the scalloped edges and the eyelets. Pipe tiny dots at each point on the outer scallop collar and at alternate points along the inside collar. Pipe around both ends of the ribbon pieces where they are 'inserted' into the cake.

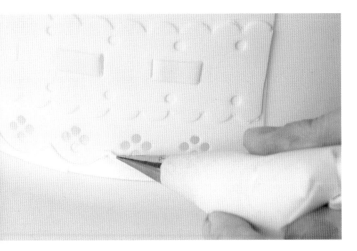

9 To make the butterfly, roll out the white flower paste until it is about 2mm (1/16in) thick. Use the butterfly cookie cutter to create the butterfly and cut it in half down the middle with a sharp knife. Trim away the body and use the eyelet cutters to make a pretty pattern on the wings. Pipe around the hole with some yellow-coloured royal icing using a no. 1 piping tube (tip).

10 When the wings are dry, make a fold down a strip of waxed paper and put it into a fold of the concertina-folded card. Put some white royal icing into a piping bag with a no. 1.5 tube (tip). Pipe a short line about 1cm (3/8in) long down the centre of the paper and stick the two 'run-out' wing shapes together. Pipe the head and body of the butterfly and leave to dry before removing it from the paper.

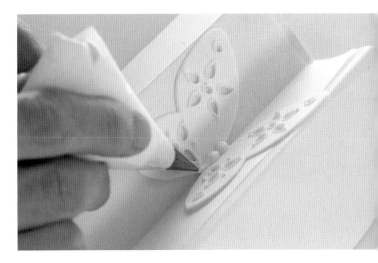

11 Finish by securing some 15mm (5/8in) white satin ribbon around the base board with double-sided tape and sticking the butterfly to the top of the cake with a small amount of royal icing.

Butterfly cupcakes

These soft, yellow buttercream-topped cupcakes surrounded by delightful broderie anglaise wrappers are so simple to create. They make the perfect accompaniment for the main cake, or are ideal for a summer party when time is short.

Fill the piping (pastry) bag with the yellow buttercream and pipe swirls on the top of each cupcake (see Decorating Cupcakes with Buttercream). Finish by wrapping each cupcake in the broderie anglaise cupcake wrappers and placing the butterflies, made in the same way as in the main project, on top.

YOU'LL ALSO NEED
* Cupcakes (flavour of choice)
* Pale yellow-coloured buttercream
* Large disposable plastic piping (pastry) bag
* Large plain piping tube (tip)
* Broderie anglaise cupcake wrappers
* Additional butterflies (see main project)

Broderie cookies

These dainty little broderie style cookies are made in a similar way to the main cake. Wrap them in cellophane, tied with a yellow ribbon, to make stunning wedding favours for your guests to cherish.

Roll out the sugarpaste until it is approximately 3–4mm ($^1/_8$in) thick and cut out the scalloped flower shape using the cookie cutter. Cut out the pattern using the no. 4 piping tube (tip) and eyelet cutter. Brush a small amount of boiled apricot jam over the cookie and stick on the sugarpaste. With yellow-coloured royal icing, pipe outlines and details around the edges and eyelets as shown for the main cake.

> **YOU'LL ALSO NEED**
> ❖ 10-petal flower-shaped cookies
> ❖ White sugarpaste
> ❖ 10-petal flower cutter
> ❖ Boiled apricot jam
> ❖ Pastry brush

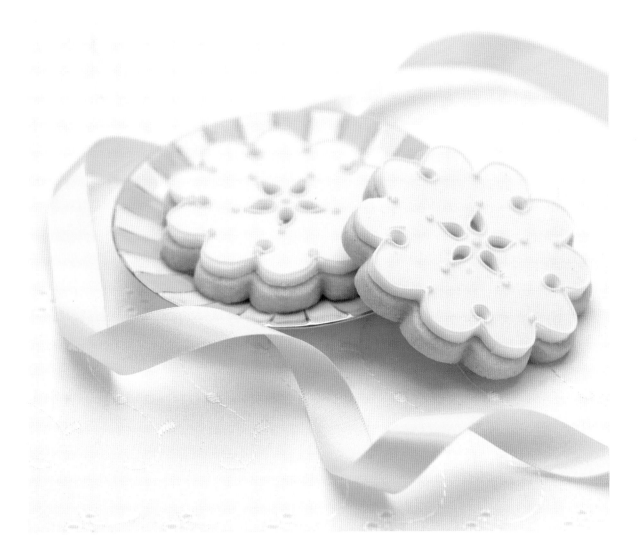

ARABIAN NIGHTS

Moroccan architecture has always fascinated me. Colour is the focal point, from shimmering shades of blue from the sea to the rich reds and oranges of African sunsets. The warm, vibrant colours and intricate patterns that can be found when wandering around Marrakesh have inspired me to bring a touch of the exotic to my sugarcraft.

These striking designs reflect the bold geometric shapes and patterns found in Moroccan architecture in beautiful detail, simply by using cutters and brightly coloured sugarpaste. They are perfect for bringing a sense of the Moroccan sunset to any summer celebration.

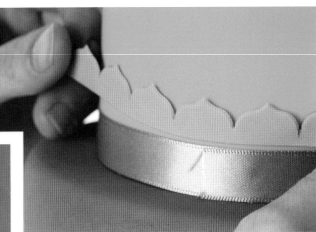

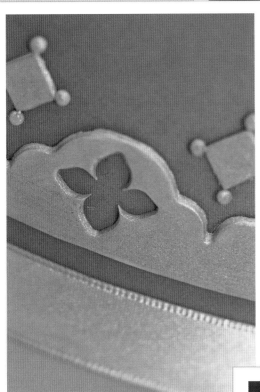

"*Vibrant colours and quiet desert shades make for an active colour palette in Moroccan design*"

Magical Marrakesh

This bold and vibrant cake design conjures up memories of the souk and the spicy air of Moroccan evenings by combining bright orange and pink colours with dusty tones as a background for the opulent gold detail. Fancy frill strips and Daphne cutters are the main shapes used to create the geometric Moroccan patterns. The iced tiers have been shaded with coloured powders to mimic the effect of old Moroccan walls.

MATERIALS

❖ One 10cm (4in) round cake, 7.5cm (3in) deep, prepared and iced in turquoise at least 12–24 hours in advance (see Baking and Covering Techniques)

❖ One 15cm (6in) round cake, 12cm (4½in) deep, prepared and iced in cerise pink at least 12–24 hours in advance

❖ One 20cm (8in) round cake, 7.5cm (3in) deep, prepared and iced in purple at least 12–24 hours in advance

❖ One 25cm (10in) round cake, 12cm (4½in) deep, covered with orange sugarpaste

❖ One 35cm (14in) round cake board covered with red sugarpaste (see Icing Cake Boards)

❖ Edible dusts: green, yellow, raspberry, aubergine, burnt orange, burgundy, gold lustre

❖ 400g (14oz) caramel-coloured flower paste

❖ Half quantity of royal icing coloured caramel

❖ Edible glue

❖ Clear alcohol

EQUIPMENT

❖ 10 hollow pieces of dowels cut to size (see Assembling Tiered Cakes)

❖ Straight frill cutters (FMM)

❖ Daphne cutter (FMM)

❖ 4cm (1½in) fuchsia cutter

❖ 2.5cm (1in) circle cutter

❖ 8–9mm (3/8in) square cutter

❖ Square eyelet cutter

❖ 15mm (5/8in) gold double-faced satin ribbon

❖ Large dusting brush

❖ Large sharp knife

❖ Small piping (pastry) bag and piping tubes (tips): nos. 1 and 4

❖ Paintbrush

❖ Double-sided tape

1 Mix the green and yellow edible dusts together to make a turquoise colour and dust it over the top tier using a large dusting brush. Repeat for the pink tier with raspberry dust, the purple tier with aubergine dust, the orange tier with burnt orange dust and the red cake board with burgundy dust.

2 Dowel and assemble the cake (see Assembling Tiered Cakes). Wrap the gold ribbon around the base of each tier and secure with double-sided tape.

3 To make the decoration on the top tier, roll out a long thin strip of the caramel flower paste to measure 30cm (12in) and use the pointed tip straight frill cutter to cut along one edge. Continue cutting the frill until you have reached either end of the paste. Cut a parallel straight edge with a large sharp knife close to the frilled edge. Stick the strip to the cake slightly above the ribbon using a small amount of edible glue. Continue around the whole tier.

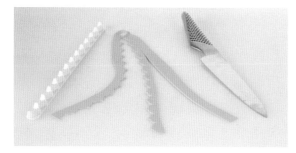

4 Roll out some more flower paste and use the small Daphne cutter to cut out the shapes above and in between the points. Cut tiny holes from the Daphnes with a no. 4 tube (tip) before sticking onto the cake.

5 Roll out another long piece of flower paste and cut long thin strips using the semi-circle frill cutter and a large sharp knife, as in Step 3. You will need enough strips to go around the bottom and top part

---TIP--------------------

If the strips are not level, use a sharp knife to move them into a position.

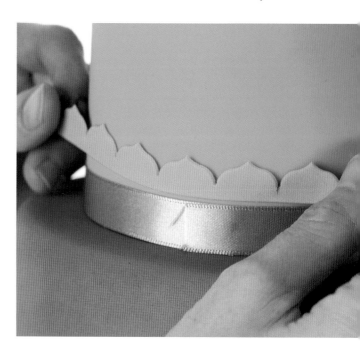

of the second pink tier. Stick them onto the cake approximately 9cm (3½in) apart. The bottom strip should stick slightly above the ribbon as before.

6 Cut circles from some more thinly rolled-out paste and cut Daphne shapes from each circle. Attach these to the 15cm (6in) cake in two evenly spaced rows between the two strips and approximately 1cm (3/8in) apart from each other. Cut out small squares and place some between the circles, positioning them at an angle like a diamond. Cut some more squares in half to make the triangles outside the circles on both sides of the straight edge of the frill strip.

7 Use the graduating scallop frill strip for the purple tier and cut out small Daphne shapes at the thickest part all the way along the icing. Cut enough strips to go around the cake and stick them onto the cake in the same way as for the other tiers. Cut more small squares to go between the points.

8 Cut some additional straight frill strips using the zigzag cutter to embellish the bottom tier. Cut enough strips to go around the bottom and the top part of the orange tier. Stick them onto the cake approximately 9cm (3½in) apart. The distance between the two strips will depend on the height of the two fuchsia shapes when placed on top of each other, allowing a little extra space for the piped dots between. Again, leave a small gap between the bottom strip and the ribbon.

9 Roll out some more flower paste and cut out the fuchsia shapes with the cutter. Use the eyelet cutter to cut out the small squares from the fuchsia shapes. Stick the four petal shapes to the cake in two horizontal rows and next to each other but leaving a tiny gap between them. Cut out more Daphnes and stick them in between the two rows of fuchsia shapes.

10 Place a no. 1 tube (tip) inside a small piping (pastry) bag and fill it with soft-peak caramel royal icing. Pipe dot details (see Piping with Royal Icing).

11 Mix some gold edible lustre dust with clear alcohol and carefully paint over the caramel flower paste and royal iced dots. Finish by securing gold satin ribbon around the base board with double-sided tape.

Moroccan mini lanterns

Picture these lanterns glowing with warmth over an Arabian sunset. These dome-shaped mini cakes really complement the bold colours and Moroccan influence of the larger cake.

Stick the half-sphere pieces of sponge onto the top of each mini cake with some buttercream and coat the outside of the cakes. Chill in the refrigerator (or freezer if you are short of time) to firm up, then cover the cakes with the different coloured icing used for the main project. Roll out thin strips of caramel flower paste to decorate the top and bottom of the cylinder shape. Cut more shapes using the cutters from the main project to make the patterns on the lanterns. Roll small balls and tiny sausages to make the loops from which the lanterns would be hung.

YOU'LL ALSO NEED
❖ 5cm (2in) round mini cakes filled and coated with buttercream (see Miniature Cakes)
❖ Half-sphere pieces of sponge, baked in 6cm (2½in) sphere silicone moulds
❖ Extra buttercream to stick and coat the half-sphere pieces of sponge

Eastern shoe cookies

These delightful Moroccan shoe cookies are extremely fun to make and you can be as creative as you like with their design. They would be a great accompaniment to a colourful glass of Moroccan tea.

Outline and flood the cookies with red, orange and cerise pink royal icing (see Royal-iced Cookies). Cut out the patterns on the shoes using the cutters from the main project. Pipe dots and tassels on the cookies with some caramel-coloured royal icing. Finish by painting the detail with gold edible lustre dust.

YOU'LL ALSO NEED
- ❖ Moroccan shoe cookies made from template (see Templates)
- ❖ Food colouring: red, orange, claret

BRIDAL BEAUTY

I wanted to create this cake in homage to my love of bridal blossoms and bows. Who could imagine that these two simple adornments would inspire so many beautiful wedding cakes? Hand in hand, they instantly transform a plain cake into a piece of elegant, feminine beauty.

By reflecting aspects of your dress in your cake design, it is easy to create a stunning centrepiece that will perfectly match your style and complement your look. This particular design was inspired by a gorgeous Oscar de la Renta dress. Its soft pure colours and gentle bridal tones make it perfect for a traditional wedding.

"By designing your wedding cake in the style of the bridal gown, the cake will look as breathtaking as the bride herself"

Bows and blossoms

This breathtaking cake has been made in hexagonal tiers, as I felt that the angular shape really lent itself to the simplicity of the blossom design and made a welcome alternative to the classic round shape. The large, soft peach bow, ruffled and draped down the cake, mirrors the gorgeous sash detail on the Oscar de la Renta dress and adds a stunning hint of colour to the cake. To create the pattern, cut the blossoms from flower paste, which is textured by pressing the paste into a lace mould or textured mat. You could alternatively run an embossing stick over them.

MATERIALS

❖ One 13cm (5in) hexagonal cake, one 18cm (7in) hexagonal cake, one 23cm (9in) hexagonal cake and one 30cm (12in) hexagonal cake, each 10cm (4in) deep, iced in ivory (see Baking and Covering Techniques)

❖ One 38cm (15in) hexagonal or round cake board covered with ivory sugarpaste (see Icing Cake Boards)

❖ One quantity of royal icing

❖ 200g (7oz) pale flesh-coloured flower paste

❖ 200g (7oz) white flower paste

❖ Ivory food colouring

❖ Pearl white edible lustre dust

❖ Edible glue

EQUIPMENT

❖ 10 hollow pieces of dowels cut to size (see Assembling Tiered Cakes)

❖ Lace moulds or textured mat

❖ Petunia cutters

❖ Five-petal blossom cutters

❖ Small stephanotis cutter

❖ Blossom plunger cutters

❖ 15mm (5/8in) ivory double-faced satin ribbon

❖ Small piping (pastry) bag and no. 1.5 piping tube (tip)

❖ Dusting brush

❖ Paintbrush

❖ Large sharp knife

❖ Kitchen towel

❖ Double-sided tape

1 Dowel and assemble the cake (see Assembling Tiered Cakes), using four dowels in the base tier and three in the second and third tiers.

2 Colour some soft-peak royal icing with ivory food colouring until it is the same colour as the sugarpaste covering the cake. Place a no. 1.5 piping tube (tip) into a small piping (pastry) bag and fill it with the icing. Pipe a 'snail trail' border (see Piping with Royal Icing) around the base of the bottom three tiers.

3 To make the bow, start by thinly rolling out some of the pale flesh-coloured flower paste to measure approximately 10cm (4in) wide and 30cm (12in) long. Brush some white lustre dust onto the icing, then ruffle it slightly on the horizontal and wrap it around the top tier so that the ends meet on one of the front sides of the cake. Trim away the excess paste.

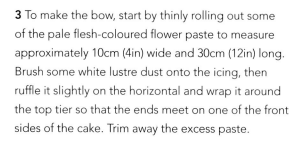

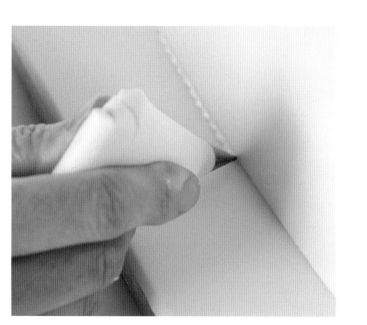

4 For the bow loops, roll out more flower paste about 20–25cm (8–10in) long and the same width as before and dust with lustre dust. Pinch the paste in the centre and at both ends and fold the ends in, sticking them to the centre with a little edible glue. Place kitchen towel inside the loops until the paste starts to dry and can almost hold its shape.

TIP

If you find working with a knife tricky, cut the paste with a sharp pair of scissors.

TIP

If the bow is still quite soft, use some more kitchen towel to help support it until it is completely dry.

5 For the knot, you will need a piece of flower paste approximately 7.5–10cm (3–4in) in length. Brush with lustre dust and ruffle as described in Step 3. Wrap the knot piece around the centre of the bow, tucking it underneath at both ends and securing it in place with a little edible glue. Set it aside to dry a little.

6 To make the two tails of the bow, roll and ruffle pieces approximately 20cm (8in) in length and brush with lustre dust as before. Trim one end of each piece on the diagonal and pinch the other end together. Stick the two tails onto the cake at the base of the top tier and let them hang naturally against the sides of the cake. Glue them in place at intervals to help support their weight. Carefully stick the bow onto the cake, using some edible glue behind the loops to help the bow stay in place.

7 To make the flowers, thinly roll out some of the white flower paste. Brush some edible lustre dust into the lace moulds or onto a textured mat and press the paste into the mould.

8 Place the paste back onto the board and cut out the different shapes using the flower and blossom cutters. Cut smaller flowers out from inside the larger flowers.

9 Stick the flowers onto the cake using some edible glue, aiming to make clusters of flowers by attaching them densely together in some areas. Finish by securing the satin ribbon around the base board using double-sided tape.

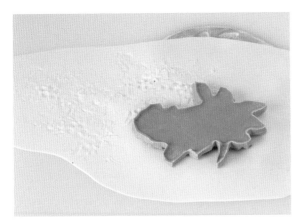

TIP

Be careful not to use too much glue, as you will leave marks on the cake where it oozes out.

Appliqué blossom cupcakes

Create an adorable wedding spread with these gorgeous little cupcakes that partner the larger cake beautifully and look lovely displayed on a tiered stand. I used the same techniques as for the main cake to create the blossoms.

Make the flowers in the same way as for the main project and stick them onto the cupcakes with some edible glue. Finish by placing the cupcakes in the pretty blossom cupcake wrappers.

YOU'LL ALSO NEED
* Domed cupcakes baked in gold foil cases (liners) and dipped in flesh-coloured fondant (see Fondant-dipped Cupcakes)
* Blossom cupcake wrappers (optional)

Beautiful bow cookies

These fantastic bow cookies are so simple to make but are guaranteed to impress your guests. They can be made well in advance, but they still look and taste wonderful for your big day, allowing you to achieve the personal touch without any last-minute stress. The bow shape ties in perfectly with the sash detail on the dress and the main cake.

Outline and flood the cookies with pale flesh-coloured royal icing (see Royal-iced Cookies). When they are dry, pipe an outline on the cookies with some more pale flesh-coloured royal icing and decorate with cut-out blossoms as shown in the main project. Cut the blossoms with a sharp knife where they would run over the edge of the cookie.

YOU'LL ALSO NEED
* Bow cookies cut with cutter
* Food colouring: flesh/paprika

PRETTY IN PINK

I love visiting flower markets in the summer months and seeing florists' buckets filled with huge heads of beautiful hydrangea, which can be found in a stunning array of colours.

The sugar hydrangeas are one of the prettiest and easiest blossoms to create for guaranteed stunning results every time. For the designs in this chapter I have used a simple buttercream base and a contemporary pink colour scheme, which would be the perfect complement to a summer wedding.

"Pink is the colour of romance and hydrangeas are one of the most romantic flowers, often seen in bridal bouquets"

Tumbling hydrangeas

The delicate little handmade hydrangeas are the main feature of this beautiful cake design. They are simply made by cutting out blossom shapes from some coloured pink paste and pressing them between a special mould. Take time when positioning your flowers – the beauty of this design is in the way the delicate pink blossoms elegantly cascade down the tiers and onto the base.

MATERIALS

❖ One 10cm (4in) round cake, one 18cm (7in) round cake, one 25cm (10in) round cake and one 33cm (13in) round cake, each approximately 10cm (4in) deep and layered, filled and covered with buttercream (see Baking and Covering Techniques)

❖ One heavy-duty round 46cm (18in) cake board or two 46cm (18in) round cake boards stuck together, covered with ivory sugarpaste (see Icing Cake Boards)

❖ 500g (1lb 2oz) flavoured buttercream of choice*

❖ 300g (10½oz) white flower paste

❖ Half quantity of royal icing

❖ Paste food colourings: claret, ruby

❖ Edible dusts: pink, raspberry

❖ White fat (shortening)

EQUIPMENT

❖ 10 hollow dowels approximately 9cm (3½in) long (see Assembling Tiered Cakes)

❖ Hydrangea cutter and veiner set (Sunflower SugarArt)

❖ 15mm (5/8in) pink satin ribbon

❖ 15mm (5/8in) ivory satin ribbon

❖ Large or medium-sized palette knife

❖ Small palette knife or cake scraper

❖ Large plate or heavy-duty turntable (optional)

❖ Crumpled foil or bumpy foam

❖ Dusting brushes

❖ Small piping (pastry) bag and no. 1 piping tube (tip)

❖ Double-sided tape

* Make sure the added flavouring doesn't affect the appearance of the cake, i.e. use oils or extracts rather than zest or vanilla pods

TIP

Wait until the cakes are cool before assembling them – otherwise it could be quite messy!

1 Begin by dowelling the cakes (see Assembling Tiered Cakes). You will need four dowels in the 33cm (13in) cake, three in the 25cm (10in) cake and three in the 18cm (7in) cake. Stick the 33cm (13in) cake onto the 46cm (18in) cake board using royal icing.

2 Assemble the four tiers of the cake, using additional buttercream between each tier to sandwich them together.

3 Using a large or medium-sized palette knife, generously smear another coating of buttercream over each tier. Work the buttercream around the cake in an even fashion until you achieve a neat and fairly smooth finish.

4 You will need two or three shades of pink flower paste for the hydrangeas. Simply add varying amounts of pink food colouring to the white paste.

5 Thinly roll out some of the flower paste and cut out the blossoms using the hydrangea cutter. Once you have cut as many flowers as you can from the paste, press each one between the veiner, using white fat (shortening) to prevent them from sticking.

TIP

It's easier to add an extra coating of buttercream around each tier if the cake is placed on a large plate so that you can turn it around easily.

6 Carefully remove each flower from the veiner and put it aside to dry on some crumpled foil or bumpy foam. You will need about 175 blossoms in total in the different shades of pink.

7 When the blossoms are dry, brush each one with edible dust. Dust some more than others so that they are all in slightly different shades, to make them look more realistic.

TIP

Try not to move the cake too far once it has all been assembled. Ideally, it should be constructed where it is going to be displayed.

8 Starting at the top, decorate the cake with the hydrangeas. They should stick directly onto the buttercream but you can use a very small amount of extra buttercream if necessary. Arrange the flowers to appear as if they are tumbling from the cake top.

9 Place a no. 1 tube (tip) in a small piping (pastry) bag and fill with white royal icing. Pipe tiny dots in the centre of each flower (see Piping with Royal Icing). Finish by securing the ivory and pink satin ribbon around the base board with double-sided tape.

Summer sensation cake

This smaller single-tiered version of the main design would make a perfect anniversary or birthday cake. I have used a pretty pink colour scheme to give a slightly different effect, but it is easy to alter the colour of the flowers as you desire to suit the occasion.

To colour the buttercream, simply add a touch of pink food colouring until you get the desired shade. Cover the cake with the buttercream, following the instructions for the main project. Use the hydrangea cutter and veiner set from the main project to cut out hydrangea blossoms from pink-tinted flower paste and dust slightly with pink edible dust. Attach all over the cake as before to create a scattered, tumbling effect.

YOU'LL ALSO NEED
❖ 23cm (9in) cake (see Basic Cake Recipes)

Fabulously floral cupcakes

These pretty little cupcakes are a lovely complement or alternative to the main cake. Display them on pretty plates or carefully place them in boxes as a gift for someone special.

Use a palette knife to pile the buttercream onto the cupcakes. Use the hydrangea cutter and veiner set from the main project to cut out hydrangea blossoms in your chosen colours and attach to the cupcakes as desired.

YOU'LL ALSO NEED
❖ Cupcakes baked in clear paper cases (liners)

BLUE SKY CELEBRATION

Bunting, in the form of triangular flags, is a popular festive decoration traditionally used at regattas and village fetes. It has seen a revival in recent years and can now be found at many events, as well as often being used to decorate children's bedrooms and kitchens.

The pretty floral patterns and pale blues and pinks used in the following projects immediately conjure up a sense of summer and would be perfect for a garden party or an outdoor wedding reception. The bunting fabric effect is achieved by cutting out attractive patterns that have been printed onto edible paper – a technique that is really simple and very effective.

"*Bunting can add a fairground feel to a party, brighten up a child's room or add the perfect finishing touch to a wedding*"

Beautiful bunting

The pale blue of the sugarpaste covering is the ideal shade to represent the summer sky. The bunting gives a celebratory feel and is created by cutting out triangular pieces of edible paper, printed with various patterns, which are then hung in a zigzag fashion across and around the cake. For this design, I have used prints by fabric designer Tanya Whelan, but you can easily collect patterns yourself to create your own unique design. If you can't get hold of any edible paper, simply cut out various shapes and patterns from flower paste.

MATERIALS

❖ One 13cm (5in) round cake and one 18cm (7in) round cake, both 9cm (3½in) deep, layered, filled and covered with pale blue sugarpaste (see Baking and Covering Techniques)

❖ One 23cm (9in) round cake, 12cm (4½in) deep, layered, filled and covered with pale blue sugarpaste

❖ One 30cm (12in) round cake board covered with pale blue sugarpaste (see Icing Cake Boards)

❖ Two A4 (US Letter) sheets of edible paper printed with your choice of patterns

❖ 200g (7oz) white flower paste

❖ 50g (1¾oz) ruby flower paste

❖ 20g (¾oz) brown flower paste

❖ Edible glue

❖ White fat (shortening)

EQUIPMENT

❖ Six hollow pieces of dowels cut to size (see Assembling Tiered Cakes)

❖ Smaller and larger triangle bunting templates (see Templates)

❖ 15mm (5/8in) pale blue double-faced satin ribbon

❖ Fresh non-toxic flower (optional)

❖ Piece of string

❖ Large pins

❖ Small sharp knife

❖ Scalpel or craft knife

❖ Fine paintbrush

❖ Sugar gun with small rectangular attachment

❖ Double-sided tape

1 To make the edible paper to be used for the bunting designs, you will firstly need to create an A4 (US Letter) -sized document including your chosen designs by scanning fabrics and patterned papers or purchasing images from the Internet. Each pattern will need to be approximately 5.75 x 5.75cm (2³/8 x 2³/8in) in size.

2 Assemble the tiered cake using dowels (see Assembling Tiered Cakes). You will need three dowels each in the middle and bottom tiers. Wrap a piece of the blue satin ribbon around the base of each tier and secure in place with double-sided tape.

3 Using the string and the large pins, mark out where the triangles of the bunting are to be positioned by marking two points opposite each other on the top edge of each tier. Position the pins and string so that they create a zigzag effect across the cake from the top to bottom tier. The string should hang down from each point.

4 Roll out some white flower paste until it is approximately 1–2mm (1/16in) thick and cut out the triangular flags using the slightly smaller template provided (see Templates). You will need approximately 38 triangles.

5 Using the string as a guide, stick the flags onto the cake to form the bunting. Only use a very small amount of edible glue initially in case you need to adjust their position to space them evenly. When they are all in place, remove the string and pins.

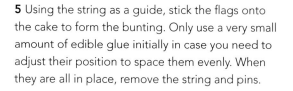

TIP

If you prefer, you can add a design to your bunting using the appliqué technique featured in the Appliqué Bunting Cookies.

6 Using the slightly larger bunting template as a guide, carefully cut out triangular pieces from the patterned edible paper with a scalpel or craft knife. Use the paper sparingly and cut out the triangles as close together as possible to prevent waste.

7 Stick the edible paper triangles onto the paste triangles using a tiny amount of edible glue applied with a fine paintbrush, allowing the paper to hang over the edges slightly.

TIP

Keep any leftover edible paper covered in a plastic sleeve to prevent it from drying out.

8 Knead a little white fat (shortening) into the ruby flower paste until it becomes elastic and use to fill the sugar gun. Lightly brush edible glue across the top of the triangles and squeeze out the paste so that it sits around the top of the bunting to create the cord.

9 Roll six tiny balls using the brown flower paste, squash them flat and stick them onto the points of the bunting to represent wooden pegs.

10 Secure blue satin ribbon around the base board with double-sided tape. A fresh flower can be used to decorate the top of the cake if desired – ensure this is non-toxic and remove before eating the cake.

Shabby chic fancies

These beautiful fancies are created by using edible paper in a similar method to the bunting in the main project. They are sure to liven up any summer garden party.

Simply cut out squares from edible paper to a similar size as the top of the fondant fancy. Stick them in place with a small amount of edible glue. Cut out small blossoms from the different coloured flower pastes using the small blossom plunger cutter and arrange them around the edges as part of the floral design.

YOU'LL ALSO NEED
- ✤ Fondant fancies dipped in pale blue and/or pink fondant, in silver cases (liners) (see Fondant Fancies)
- ✤ Flower paste: white, pale pink, ruby pink
- ✤ Small blossom plunger cutter

Appliqué bunting cookies

These triangular cookies use the same romantic colour scheme as the main project. They are made using an easy appliqué technique – cutting out various shapes from flower paste and sticking them directly onto the cookie to form a pattern. This technique gives a textured, fabric-like effect that could also be adapted for use in the main project.

Use a no. 4 piping tube (tip) to cut out tiny dots from white flower paste for the dotty flags. Cut out blossoms and leaves using different coloured pastes to make the floral cookies.

YOU'LL ALSO NEED

❖ Triangular cookies, iced in white and shades of pink (see Templates)
❖ Flower paste: pale, medium and deep pink, green, white
❖ No. 4 piping tube (tip)
❖ Blossom cutters
❖ Tiny teardrop cutters

CARNIVAL TIME

My passion for Italian tradition began while living in northern Italy. During my time spent there, I visited Venice on many occasions and was enchanted by the romanticism of the city and the magic of the Venetian carnival. It inspired me to recreate the decadence and nostalgia of Venice by focusing on the masquerade with these bold designs.

I have used a chic red, gold and black colour scheme to depict the ornate detail of the masks, which conjure up ideas of flamboyance and mystery, leaving one guessing what they are trying to hide. These designs are sure to add a sense of glamour and elegance to a ball or fancy dress party.

"Nothing beats the drama and mystery of wearing a masquerade mask to a masked ball"

Venetian masquerade

The slender, concave shape of this tiered design adds an appropriate contrast to the classic straight-edged cake, adding to the theatrical elegance of the Venetian masquerade. The ornate handcrafted sugar mask is cut using a template and then moulded and left to dry over a real mask to take on the same shape.

MATERIALS

❖ One 13cm (5in) round sponge cake, 10cm (4in) deep, made from three layers of sponge (see Baking and Covering Techniques)

❖ One 20cm (8in) round sponge cake, 15cm (6in) deep, made from four layers of sponge

❖ One 28cm (11in) round cake board, iced in black sugarpaste (see Icing Cake Boards)

❖ One 10cm (4in), 3mm (1/8in) cake board

❖ One 15cm (6in) cake board

❖ One quantity of buttercream, flavour of choice

❖ 300g (10½oz) caramel-coloured flower paste

❖ 500g (1lb 2oz) black sugarpaste

❖ 750g (1lb 10oz) white sugarpaste

❖ 200g (7oz) black flower paste

❖ One quantity of royal icing

❖ 200g (7oz) red modelling paste

❖ 100g (3½oz) red flower paste

❖ Ivory paste food colouring

❖ Gold spray

❖ Gold edible lustre dust

❖ Edible glue

❖ White fat (shortening)

❖ Clear alcohol

EQUIPMENT

❖ Mask template (see Templates)

❖ Plain real life-sized mask (you can buy masks online or from a good fancy dress shop)

❖ Three hollow pieces of dowels cut to size (see Assembling Tiered Cakes)

❖ Large swag and tassel mould

❖ Jewel mould (Squire's Kitchen Shop)

❖ Black wired feather

❖ 15mm (5/8in) black double-faced satin ribbon

❖ Gold trim (optional)

❖ Large serrated knife

❖ Small sharp knife

❖ Scalpel or craft knife

❖ Clear plastic sleeve

❖ Small piping (pastry) bags and no. 1.5 piping tube (tip)

❖ Paintbrush

❖ Double-sided tape

1 Begin by carving the top tier. Place the 10cm (4in) cake board in the centre of the cake and carefully cut downwards from the board to the outer 13cm (5in) base to create a slanted edge around the cake. Turn the cake up the right way and fill and coat the outside as usual (see Baking and Covering Techniques). Place in the refrigerator to firm up for at least half an hour.

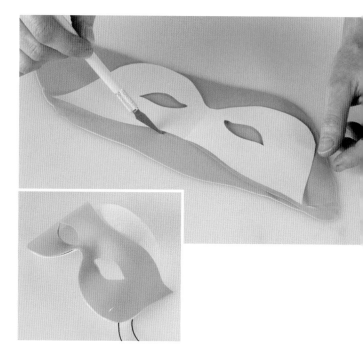

2 Repeat this process for the 20cm (8in) tier using the 15cm (6in) cake board as a guide for the base of the cake. This cake can be stuck straight onto the centre of the 28cm (11in) cake board with some buttercream. Place it in the refrigerator with the top tier.

TIP

When covering the cakes, be careful that the icing doesn't tear around the top edge.

3 To make the mask, roll out 150g (5½oz) of caramel-coloured flower paste large enough to fit the mask template and about 1–2mm (1/16in) thick. Cut around the template with a small sharp knife or scalpel or craft knife, carefully sit the icing over the real mask mould and set aside to dry. When dry, remove the mask from the mould and decorate with gold spray. Put the mask back on the mould until you are ready to decorate it.

4 Knead the black and white sugarpaste together to make a dark charcoal grey colour and cover both cakes (see Baking and Covering Techniques). Use your hands to cup the icing slightly upwards before smoothing it down to the base.

5 Dowel the bottom tier (see Assembling Tiered Cakes) and carefully stack on the top tier, sticking it firmly in place with some royal icing.

6 Thinly roll out some more caramel-coloured flower paste and place it under a plastic sleeve while you roll out the black flower paste.

7 Cut strips of paste from both colours to go around the base of each cake, using a template if required. They need to be long enough to come approximately two-thirds of the way up the side of the cake. The stripes around the bottom tier are approximately 2.5cm (1in) thick and the stripes around the top tier about 1.25cm (½in) thick. Stick the strips one at a time, alternating each colour, onto the cake with a small amount of edible glue. The bottom of the strip will be slightly narrower than the top because of the slanted edge of the cake.

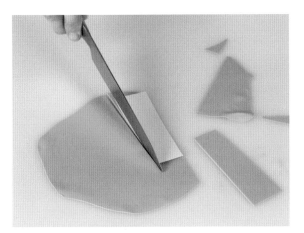

TIP

For a neat result, trim each piece of icing as you go using a small sharp knife.

8 Colour a small amount of royal icing with ivory paste colouring to make a caramel colour. Place a no. 1.5 tube (tip) in a small piping (pastry) bag and fill it with the icing. Pipe a 'snail trail' line around the top edge of the stripes (see Piping with Royal Icing).

9 Lightly grease the swag mould and press some of the red modelling paste inside to take on the shape. Attach the swags around the cake with some edible glue. Press the leftover caramel-coloured flower paste into the tassel mould and stick them on the cake where the swags come to a point and meet each other.

10 Thinly roll out the red flower paste and cut a piece measuring approximately 18cm (7in) square. Gather up the icing and drape it over the top tier so that it hangs slightly off the front edge like a piece of fabric. Use some of the red modelling paste to go under the flower paste to create a little height if necessary.

11 To decorate the mask, press some black flower paste into the jewel mould, greased with some white fat (shortening). Stick the jewel onto the mask with some edible glue and pipe a scroll border around the outside edge, the eyes and the jewel with some more caramel-coloured royal icing.

12 Paint the caramel stripes, 'snail trail' border, swags and mask detailing with gold lustre dust mixed with a small amount of clear alcohol. Attach the black feather with some royal icing at the back of the mask. Secure black satin ribbon around the base board with double-sided tape, topped with gold trim, if you like.

Masked beauty cupcakes

Bring some theatrics to the party with these decorative little cupcakes, which beautifully echo the opulence of the main cake. Add variety to the cakes by experimenting with your own different-shaped mask templates.

Thinly roll out square pieces of red flower paste and drape them over the cupcakes so that they hang slightly off one edge, using a little edible glue to hold them in place. Make the masks in the same way as the mask on the main cake and set them aside to dry on foam, scrunched-up tissue or foil. Pipe the detail on the mask with royal icing and paint it gold. Stick the masks onto the cupcakes using a small amount of royal icing.

YOU'LL ALSO NEED
- ❖ Charcoal-coloured, fondant-dipped cupcakes (see Fondant-dipped Cupcakes)
- ❖ Small mask templates (see Templates)
- ❖ Foam, tissue or foil

Feathered fan cookies

Set the scene for your very own Venetian table spread with these ornate fan cookies. They are a perfect accompaniment to the masked cakes and give a different angle to the carnival theme.

Roll out black and caramel-coloured sugarpaste and cut out the fans from both colours. Using the circle cutter, cut the top of the fan from the black icing and the bottom from the caramel. Fit the pieces together on the surface before sticking them onto the cookie with apricot jam. Mark the indentations using a cocktail stick (toothpick) around the bottom third of the fan and a paintbrush around the rest. Mark the feather detail in the black sugarpaste with the end of a paintbrush. Pipe the detail with caramel-coloured royal icing and paint with gold lustre dust when dry.

YOU'LL ALSO NEED
- ✤ Fan-shaped cookies
- ✤ Caramel-coloured sugarpaste
- ✤ Fan cookie cutter
- ✤ 7–8cm (2¾–3¼in) circle cutter
- ✤ Apricot jam
- ✤ Cocktail stick (toothpick)

WINTER WONDERLAND

Adorned with delicate showers of snowflakes, this frosty collection of bijoux cakes rightfully belongs in a winter wonderland. Soft neutral tones are a real must this winter and they marry beautifully with the glitzy sparkle of the snowflakes. These crisp designs would make sparkling centrepieces for a winter wedding or festive celebration.

I have used two different techniques to create the decoration on these cakes, adding contrast and definition. The delicate metallics and icy glitters make the snowflakes really stand proud. By using a variety of cutters and decoration, it is easy to make each cake as individual as the snowflakes themselves.

"The real beauty of snowflakes is that every one is unique in its individuality"

Sparkling tower

This beautiful tower of glistening, snowflake-adorned mini cakes is perfect for any winter party or wedding. The use of a neutral colour scheme really makes this stand out from other winter designs, and could easily complement a bridal colour scheme. You could give the mini cakes to your guests as gifts or favours, or for a smaller occasion, use the top tier as a stand-alone cake.

MATERIALS

❖ One 10cm (4in) and one 15cm (6in) round cake, each 9cm (3½in) deep, iced in pale grey (see Baking and Covering Techniques)

❖ 32 miniature cakes: 5 x 5cm (2 x 2in), iced in pale grey, white, ivory and latte (see Miniature Cakes)

❖ 400–500g (14oz–1lb 2oz) white flower paste

❖ One quantity of royal icing

❖ Food colourings: black, brown, ivory

❖ Edible lustre dust: pearl white, silver snow, pearlized toffee, ivory pearl

❖ Glitters: white diamond, cream diamond, disco silver, disco champagne

❖ Edible glue

❖ White fat (shortening)

❖ Clear alcohol

EQUIPMENT

❖ Three hollow pieces of dowels cut to size (see Assembling Tiered Cakes)

❖ Decorative strip cutter (FMM)

❖ Snowflake stencil

❖ Snowflake cutters (Lindy's Cakes)

❖ Small teardrop cutter

❖ Small circle cutter

❖ Small diamond cutter

❖ Large sharp knife

❖ Dusting brush

❖ Acetate

❖ Small piping (pastry) bags and piping tubes (tips): nos. 1.5, 3 and 4

❖ Paintbrush

❖ Perspex cake stand

1 Dowel and assemble the 10cm (4in) and 15cm (6in) cakes (see Assembling Tiered Cakes).

2 Thinly roll out a long strip of white flower paste. Using the strip cutter and a large sharp knife, cut out two borders to decorate the base of both tiers. Dust some pearl white edible lustre dust over the strips of icing before sticking them in place with a small amount of edible glue. You may need to use a couple of pieces to go around the 15cm (6in) tier.

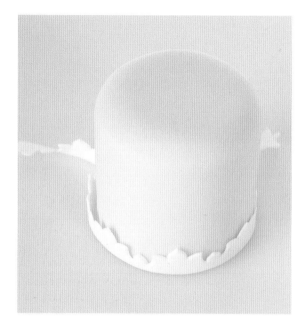

3 Make a trim to go around each miniature cake. The pale grey cakes are decorated with pearl white borders as for the two-tier top cake, the white cakes are decorated with grey strips of flower paste dusted with silver snow, the ivory cakes are decorated with latte-coloured flower paste dusted with pearlized toffee and the latte-coloured cakes are decorated with ivory flower paste and ivory pearl dust.

4 To make the small glitter snowflakes, place the snowflake stencil on top of some acetate, lightly greased with white fat (shortening), and thinly smear some fairly stiff royal icing over the top until the stencil sheet is covered. Carefully lift off the stencil and sprinkle on some white diamond glitter before the icing starts to dry out.

5 Repeat this using ivory-coloured icing and cream diamond glitter, grey icing and disco silver glitter, and latte-coloured icing and disco champagne glitter.

6 The larger snowflakes are cut from white, grey, ivory and latte-coloured flower paste using the snowflake cutters. Cut out the main snowflake shape, then use the small teardrop, circle and diamond cutters and the no. 4 piping tube (tip) to make more delicate and intricate designs.

7 Using a no. 1.5 piping tube (tip), pipe little dots of royal icing onto the points of some of the snowflakes, laid on a sheet of acetate, to make them more interesting (see Piping with Royal Icing). Leave to dry. You will need approximately 30–40 snowflakes.

8 To make the snowflakes shine, paint them with lustre dust mixed with clear alcohol. Use the same coloured lustres for each coloured snowflake as you did for the pretty borders around each cake. Leave to dry.

9 Carefully stick the snowflakes randomly onto the tiered cake and mini cakes with some royal icing. Fill the Perspex stand with the cakes and place the two-tier top cake on top. You can stick any leftover snowflakes onto the stand for extra sparkle and shine.

TIP

When assembling the tiers, I have kept the golden/ivory colour tones separate from the silver and white tones, but you could mix them up if you prefer.

Little winter wonder

This cute mini version of the main top cake is easy to create, as dowelling is not required between the two tiers. The results are simple and stunning, and it makes a gorgeous gift to give to someone special at Christmas time.

Attach the 5cm (2in) cake on top of the 7.5cm (3in) cake using some royal icing. There is no need to dowel the cake. Make the border around the base of both tiers in the same way as for the main project and decorate with snowflakes.

Frosted snowflake cookies

These glistening snowflake cookies are wonderfully simple and effective – great for any winter occasion or to adorn your Christmas tree. They are extremely versatile and you can make them truly unique by experimenting with different colours and adding ribbons. Here I have used edible flakes and glitter to add extra texture and sparkle.

Mix together equal quantities of clear glitter flakes and white diamond glitter. One at a time, outline and flood the cookies with ivory royal icing (see Royal-iced Cookies). Immediately sprinkle them with the glitter flakes before the icing starts to dry. Let the icing dry completely before shaking off the excess glitter. Embellish with ribbon if desired.

YOU'LL ALSO NEED
❖ Snowflake cookies
❖ Clear glitter flakes
❖ Ribbon (optional)

Recipes and techniques

CAKE RECIPES

It's important that your cake tastes as good as it looks. Always try to use the finest ingredients that you can find, as this will make a big difference to the flavour. In order to achieve a professional, crust-free result, bake your cake in a tin 2.5cm (1in) bigger than the actual size you would like your finished cake to be. The sizes and quantities specified in the charts on the following pages will make cakes about 9cm (3½in) deep. For shallower cakes, miniature cakes and fondant fancies, use smaller quantities (see Miniature Cakes and Fondant Fancies). For larger cakes, you will need to make two batches of the mixture. For many of the projects you can use any of the following cake recipes.

EQUIPMENT FOR CAKE MAKING

- ❖ Greaseproof (wax) paper or baking parchment and tins
- ❖ Kitchen scales
- ❖ Measuring spoons and jug (pitcher)
- ❖ Large electric mixer
- ❖ 2–3 mixing bowls in different sizes
- ❖ Sieve (strainer)
- ❖ Spatula
- ❖ Palette knife
- ❖ Metal skewer
- ❖ Saucepan
- ❖ Large metal spoon
- ❖ Clingfilm (plastic wrap)

CLASSIC SPONGE CAKE

For a really light sponge cake, it is better to separate the mixture between two tins. If you want three layers for your cake, split the mixture one-third/two-thirds. For smaller cakes, you can also cut three layers of sponge from a larger square cake. For example a 15cm (6in) round can be cut from a 30cm (12in) square cake (see opposite).

1 Preheat your oven to 160°C/325°F/Gas Mark 3 and line your tins (see Preparing Cake Tins).

2 In a large electric mixer, beat the butter and sugar together until light and fluffy. Add the eggs gradually, beating well between each addition, then add the flavouring.

TIP

Make sure that the butter and eggs you are using are at room temperature before you start.

3 Sift the flour, add to the mixture and mix very carefully until just combined.

4 Remove the mixing bowl from the mixer and fold the mixture through gently with a spatula to finish. Tip the mixture into your prepared tin or tins and spread with a palette knife or the back of a spoon.

5 Bake in the oven until a skewer inserted into the centre of your cakes comes out clean. The baking time will vary depending on your oven. Check small cakes after 20 minutes and larger cakes after 40 minutes.

6 Allow to cool, then wrap the cake well in clingfilm (plastic wrap) and refrigerate until ready to use.

If cutting three layers from a larger square cake: for a 15cm (6in) round cake, bake an 8-egg/400g (14oz) butter etc. mix in a 30cm (12in) square tin; for a 13cm (5in) round or square cake, bake a 7-egg/350g (12oz) mix in a 28cm (11in) square tin; for a 10cm (4in) round or square cake, bake a 6-egg/300g (10½oz) mix in a 25cm (10in) square tin. For sculpted and carved cakes, add 10 per cent extra flour.

Additional flavourings

For the classic sponge cake:

Lemon Add the finely grated zest of 1 lemon per 100g (3½oz) sugar.

Orange Add the finely grated zest of 2 oranges per 250g (9oz) sugar.

Chocolate Replace 10g (¼oz) flour with 10g (¼oz) cocoa powder (unsweetened cocoa) per 100g (3½oz) flour.

Banana Replace the caster (superfine) sugar with brown sugar. Add 1 overripe, mashed banana and ½ teaspoon mixed spice (apple pie spice) per 100g (3½oz) flour.

Cake size	13cm (5in) round / 10cm (4in) square	15cm (6in) round / 13cm (5in) square	18cm (7in) round / 15cm (6in) square	20cm (8in) round / 18cm (7in) square	23cm (9in) round / 20cm (8in) square	25cm (10in) round / 23cm (9in) square	28cm (11in) round / 25cm (10in) square	30cm (12in) round / 28cm (11in) square	33cm (13in) round / 20cm (12in) square
Unsalted butter	150g (5½oz)	200g (7oz)	250g (9oz)	325g (11½oz)	450g (1lb)	525g (1lb 3oz)	625g (1lb 6oz)	800g (1lb 12oz)	1kg (2lb 4oz)
Caster (superfine) sugar	150g (5½oz)	200g (7oz)	250g (9oz)	325g (11½oz)	450g (1lb)	525g (1lb 3oz)	625g (1lb 6oz)	800g (1lb 12oz)	1kg (2lb 4oz)
Medium eggs	3	4	5	6	9	10	12	14	17
Vanilla extract (tsp)	½	1	1	1½	2	2	2½	4	4½
Self-raising (-rising) flour	150g (5½oz)	200g (7oz)	250g (9oz)	325g (11½oz)	450g (1lb)	525g (1lb 3oz)	625g (1lb 6oz)	800g (1lb 12oz)	1kg (2lb 4oz)

CLASSIC CHOCOLATE CAKE

This chocolate cake recipe is really quick and easy to make and has a lovely light texture. You should split the cake mixture between two tins, either dividing it equally or into one-third and two-thirds for three-layered cakes. Use a chocolate ganache filling rather than buttercream for a richer, more indulgent flavour (see Ganache).

1 Preheat your oven to 160°C/325°F/Gas Mark 3 and line your tins (see Preparing Cake Tins).

2 Sift the flour, cocoa powder (unsweetened cocoa) and baking powder together.

3 In a large electric mixer, beat the butter and sugar together until light and fluffy. Meanwhile, crack your eggs into a separate bowl.

4 Add the eggs to the mixture gradually, beating well between each addition.

5 Add half the dry ingredients and mix until just combined before adding half the milk. Repeat with the remaining ingredients. Mix until the mixture starts to come together.

6 Finish mixing the ingredients together by hand with a spatula and spoon into your prepared tins.

7 Bake in the oven until a skewer inserted into the centre of your cakes comes out clean. The baking time will vary depending on your oven. Check smaller cakes after 20 minutes and larger cakes after 40 minutes.

8 Leave to cool, then wrap the cakes well in clingfilm (plastic wrap) and refrigerate until ready to use.

Cake size	13cm (5in) round / 10cm (4in) square	15cm (6in) round / 13cm (5in) square	18cm (7in) round / 15cm (6in) square	20cm (8in) round / 18cm (7in) square	23cm (9in) round / 20cm (8in) square	25cm (10in) round / 23cm (9in) square	28cm (11in) round / 25cm (10in) square	30cm (12in) round / 28cm (11in) square	33cm (13in) round / 20cm (12in) square
Plain (all-purpose) flour	170g (6oz)	225g (8oz)	280g (10oz)	365g (12½oz)	500g (1lb 2oz)	585g (1lb 4½oz)	700g (1lb 9oz)	825g (1lb 13oz)	1kg (2lb 4oz)
Cocoa powder (unsweetened cocoa)	30g (1oz)	40g (1½oz)	50g (1¾oz)	65g (2¼oz)	90g (3¼oz)	100g (3½oz)	125g (4½oz)	150g (5½oz)	185g (6½oz)
Baking powder (teaspoons)	1½	2	2½	3¼	4½	5¼	6¼	7½	9¼
Unsalted butter	150g (5½oz)	200g (7oz)	250g (9oz)	325g (11½oz)	450g (1lb)	525g (1lb 3oz)	625g (1lb 6oz)	750g (1lb 10oz)	925g (2lb 1oz)
Caster (superfine) sugar	130g (4½oz)	175g (6oz)	220g (8oz)	285g (10oz)	400g (14oz)	460g (1lb 1oz)	550g (1lb 4oz)	650g (1lb 7oz)	960g (2lb 2oz)
Large eggs	2½	3	4	5	7	8½	10	12	15
Full-fat (whole) milk	100ml (3½fl oz)	135ml (4½fl oz)	170ml (5¾fl oz)	220ml (8fl oz)	300ml (10fl oz)	350ml (12fl oz)	425ml (15fl oz)	500ml (18fl oz)	765ml (1 pint 7fl oz)

Additional flavourings

For the classic chocolate cake:

Orange Use the finely grated zest of 1 orange per 2 eggs.

Coffee liqueur Add 1 shot of cooled espresso coffee per 2–3 eggs and add coffee liqueur to taste to the sugar syrup (see Sugar Syrup).

Chocolate hazelnut Replace 10 per cent of the flour with the same quantity of ground hazelnuts and layer with chocolate hazelnut spread and ganache (see Ganache).

CARROT CAKE

Grated carrot and chopped pecan nuts give this recipe a lovely texture as well as a divine taste. I prefer to have only two layers of carrot cake sandwiched together with one layer of buttercream to make up one tier, so for the best results divide the quantities listed opposite between two tins to bake them. Lemon-flavoured buttercream is my favourite choice of filling, as it complements the cake perfectly.

1 Preheat the oven to 160°C/325°F/Gas Mark 3 and line your tins (see Preparing Cake Tins).

2 In a large mixer, beat together the sugar and vegetable oil for about a minute until the mixture is well combined.

3 Crack your eggs into a bowl and add them to the mixture one at a time, beating well between each addition.

4 Sift together the dry ingredients and add them to the cake mixture, alternating with the grated carrot.

5 Fold in the chopped nuts.

6 Divide the mixture between two prepared tins and bake in the oven for 20–50 minutes, depending on size. Check that the cake is cooked by inserting a skewer into the centre, which should come out clean.

7 Leave to cool, then wrap the cakes well in clingfilm (plastic wrap) and refrigerate until ready to use.

TIP

You can replace the pecans with walnuts, hazelnuts or a mixture of nuts, if you prefer.

Cake size	13cm (5in) round 10cm (4in) square	15cm (6in) round 13cm (5in) square	18cm (7in) round 15cm (6in) square	20cm (8in) round 18cm (7in) square	23cm (9in) round 20cm (8in) square	25cm (10in) round 23cm (9in) square	28cm (11in) round 25cm (10in) square	30cm (12in) round 28cm (11in) square	33cm (13in) round 20cm (12in) square
Brown sugar	135g (4¾oz)	180g (6oz)	250g (9oz)	320g (11½oz)	385g (13¼oz)	525g (1lb 3oz)	560g (1lb 4½oz)	735g (1lb 9½oz)	900g (2lb)
Vegetable oil	135ml (4½fl oz)	180ml (6¼fl oz)	250ml (9fl oz)	320ml (10¼fl oz)	385ml (13¼fl oz)	525ml (18½fl oz)	560ml (1 pint)	735ml (1 pint 6fl oz)	900ml (1 pint 12fl oz)
Medium eggs	2	2½	3	4	5	6½	7	9	11
Self-raising (-rising) flour	200g (7oz)	275g (9½oz)	375g (13oz)	480g (1lb 1oz)	590g (1lb 5oz)	775g (1lb 11oz)	850g (1lb 14oz)	1.1kg (2lb 7oz)	1.35kg (3lb 2oz)
Mixed spice (apple pie spice) (tbsp)	1	1½	2	2½	3	4	4½	5½	5¾
Bicarbonate of soda (baking soda) (tsp)	¼	½	¾	¾	1	1	1¼	1½	2
Finely grated carrot	300g (10½oz)	385g (13½oz)	525g (1lb 3oz)	675g (1lb 8oz)	825g (1lb 13oz)	1.05g (2lb 4oz)	1.2kg (2lb 11oz)	1.5kg (3lb 5oz)	1.8kg (4lb)
Finely chopped pecans	65g (2½oz)	85g (3oz)	120g (4¼oz)	150g (5½oz)	175g (6oz)	240g (8¾oz)	270g (9½oz)	350g (12oz)	425g (15oz)

TRADITIONAL FRUIT CAKE

I have made many fruit cake recipes over the years, and this is one of my favourite ones. You can replace the dried fruits with other dried fruits of your choice or keep it simple by using only pre-mixed dried fruit. Choose different types of alcohol to flavour your cake according to your own taste – I like to use equal quantities of cherry brandy and plain brandy. Rum, sherry and whisky also work well.

   You need to soak your dried fruit and mixed peel in the alcohol at least 24 hours in advance. Ideally, your cake needs to be baked at least one month before it is to be eaten to allow it time to mature. You can also 'feed' your cake with alcohol once a week to keep the cake really moist and to enhance its flavour.

1 Preheat your oven to 150°C/300°F/Gas Mark 2 and line your tin with two layers of greaseproof (wax) paper or baking parchment for small cakes, and three layers for larger cakes (see Preparing Cake Tins).

2 In a large electric mixer, beat the butter and sugar together with the lemon and orange zest until fairly light and fluffy. Add the orange juice to the soaked fruit and mixed peel.

TIP

For a large fruit cake, once you have incorporated the eggs, you may need to transfer the mixture to a large bowl to mix in the remaining ingredients.

TIP

Make sure that the lining extends beyond the rim because standard cake tins are usually only 7.5cm (3in) deep and the cake will probably rise a little above the rim.

3 Gradually add your eggs, one at a time, beating well between each addition.

4 Sift the flour and spices together and add half the flour mixture together with half the soaked fruit mixture to the cake mixture. Mix until just combined and then add the remaining flour mixture and fruit mixture.

5 Gently fold in the almonds and treacle (molasses) with a large metal spoon until all the ingredients are combined and then spoon the mixture into your prepared baking tin.

6 Cover the top loosely with some more greaseproof (wax) paper or baking parchment and then bake in the oven for the time indicated or until a skewer inserted into the centre comes out clean.

7 Pour some more alcohol over the cake while it is hot and leave to cool in the tin.

8 Remove from the tin and wrap your cake in a layer of greaseproof (wax) paper and then foil to store.

Cake size	10cm (4in) round	13cm (5in) round 10cm (4in) square	15cm (6in) round 13cm (5in) square	18cm (7in) round 15cm (6in) square	20cm (8in) round 18cm (7in) square	23cm (9in) round 20cm (8in) square	25cm (10in) round 23cm (9in) square	28cm (11in) round 25cm (10in) square	30cm (12in) round 28cm (11in) square
Currants	100g (3½oz)	125g (4½oz)	175g (6oz)	225g (8oz)	300g (10½oz)	375g (13oz)	450g (1lb)	550g (1lb 4oz)	660g (1lb 7oz)
Raisins	125g (4½oz)	150g (5½oz)	200g (7oz)	275g (9½oz)	350g (12oz)	450g (1lb)	555g (1lb 4oz)	675g (1lb 8oz)	800g (1lb 12oz)
Sultanas (golden raisins)	125g (4½oz)	150g (5½oz)	200g (7oz)	275g (9½oz)	350g (12oz)	450g (1lb)	555g (1lb 4oz)	675g (1lb 8oz)	800g (1lb 12oz)
Glacé (candied) cherries	40g (1½oz)	50g (1¾oz)	70g (2½oz)	100g (3½oz)	125g (4½oz)	150g (5½oz)	180g (6oz)	200g (7oz)	250g (9oz)
Mixed peel	25g (1oz)	30g (1oz)	45g (1¾oz)	50g (1¾oz)	70g (2½oz)	85g (3oz)	110g (3¾oz)	125g (4½oz)	150g (5½oz)
Cherry brandy and brandy mix (tbsp)	2	2½	3	3½	5	6	7	8	9
Slightly salted butter	100g (3½oz)	125g (4½oz)	175g (6oz)	225g (8oz)	350g (12oz)	375g (13oz)	450g (1lb)	550g (1lb 4oz)	660g (1lb 7oz)
Brown sugar	100g (3½oz)	125g (4½oz)	175g (6oz)	225g (8oz)	350g (12oz)	375g (13oz)	450g (1lb)	550g (1lb 4oz)	660g (1lb 7oz)
Grated zest of lemon (per fruit)	¼	½	¾	1	1½	1¾	2	2½	3
Grated zest of small orange (per fruit)	¼	½	¾	1	1½	1¾	2	2½	3
Juice of small orange (per fruit)	¼	¼	½	½	¾	¾	1	1½	1½
Medium eggs	2	2½	3	4½	6	7	8½	10	12
Plain (all-purpose) flour	100g (3½oz)	125g (4½oz)	175g (6oz)	225g (8oz)	350g (12oz)	375g (13oz)	450g (1lb)	550g (1lb 4oz)	660g (1lb 7oz)
Mixed spice (apple pie spice) (tsp)	½	½	¾	¾	1	1¼	1½	1½	1¾
Ground nutmeg (tsp)	¼	¼	½	½	½	¾	¾	1	1
Ground almonds	10g (¼oz)	15g (½oz)	20g (¾oz)	25g (1oz)	35g (1¼oz)	45g (1½oz)	55g (2oz)	65g (2½oz)	75g (2¾oz)
Flaked (slivered) almonds	10g (¼oz)	15g (½oz)	20g (¾oz)	25g (1oz)	35g (1¼oz)	45g (1½oz)	55g (2oz)	65g (2½oz)	75g (2¾oz)
Black treacle (molasses) (tbsp)	½	¾	1	1½	1½	1¾	2	2½	3
Baking time (hours)	2½	2¾	3	3½	4	4½	4¾	5½	6

FILLINGS & COVERINGS

Fillings are used to add flavour and moisture to a cake and should complement the sponge mixture. Buttercream and flavoured ganache are the two most widely used fillings and both recipes here allow cakes to be stored at room temperature so that they can be safely displayed rather than having to keep them in the refrigerator until ready to be eaten. Ganache is usually used for chocolate-flavoured cakes.

Buttercream and ganache are also used to seal and coat the cake before icing. They make a firm and perfectly smooth surface for the icing to sit on, filling in any gaps and imperfections in the cake.

BUTTERCREAM

Makes about 500g (1lb 2oz), enough for an 18–20cm (7–8in) round or square layered cake, or 20–24 cupcakes

MATERIALS

❖ 170g (6oz) unsalted or slightly salted butter, softened

❖ 340g (11¾oz) icing (confectioners') sugar

❖ 2 tablespoons water

❖ 1 teaspoon vanilla extract or alternative flavouring (see left)

EQUIPMENT

❖ Electric mixer

❖ Spatula

1 Put the butter and icing (confectioners') sugar in the bowl of an electric mixer and mix together, starting on a low speed to prevent the mixture from going everywhere.

2 Add the water and vanilla extract or other flavouring and increase the speed, beating the buttercream really well until it becomes pale, light and fluffy.

3 Store the buttercream for up to two weeks in the refrigerator in an airtight container.

Flavour variations

Lemon Add the finely grated zest of 1 lemon
Orange Add the finely grated zest of 1 orange
Chocolate Stir in 90g (3¼oz) melted white, milk or dark (semisweet or bittersweet) chocolate
Passion fruit Stir in 1 teaspoon strained and reduced passion fruit pulp
Coffee Add 1 teaspoon coffee extract
Almond Add a few drops of almond extract or to taste
Jams and conserves (jellies and preserves) can also be mixed in or used on top of a layer of buttercream, for example vanilla buttercream and raspberry jam filling.

GANACHE

This rich, smooth filling is made from chocolate and cream. It is important to use good-quality chocolate, with at least 53 per cent cocoa solids, in order to achieve the best result.

Makes about 500g (1lb 2oz), enough for an 18–20cm (7–8in) round or square layered cake, or 20–24 cupcakes

MATERIALS

* 250g (9oz) dark (semisweet or bittersweet) chocolate, chopped, or callets
* 250g (9oz) double (heavy) cream

EQUIPMENT

* Saucepan
* Mixing bowl
* Spatula

1 Put the chocolate in a bowl.

2 Bring the cream to the boil in a saucepan, then pour over the chocolate.

3 Stir until the chocolate has all melted and is perfectly combined with the cream. Leave to cool and cover.

4 Store for up to a week in the refrigerator.

TIP

Make sure that your ganache or buttercream is at room temperature before you use it – you may even need to warm it slightly so that it spreads easily.

White chocolate ganache

White chocolate ganache is a nice alternative to buttercream for heavy sponge cake fillings (cakes that have been made with extra flour). Use white chocolate in place of the dark (semisweet or bittersweet) chocolate and half the amount of cream. If you are making a small batch, melt the white chocolate before mixing with the hot cream.

SUGAR SYRUP

This is brushed onto the sponge to add moisture and flavour. The amount of syrup used is a personal choice. If you feel that your cake is quite dry, use more syrup. However, be aware that if you add too much syrup, your cake can become overly sweet and sticky. I recommend the following quantities for a 20cm (8in) layered round cake (you will need slightly more for a 20cm/8in square cake), 25 fondant fancies or 20–24 cupcakes.

MATERIALS

❖ 80g (3oz) caster (superfine) sugar
❖ 80ml (2³/4fl oz) water
❖ Flavouring (optional – see below left)

EQUIPMENT

❖ Saucepan
❖ Metal spoon

1 Put the sugar and water in a saucepan and bring to the boil, stirring once or twice.

2 Add any flavouring and leave to cool. Store in an airtight container in the refrigerator for up to one month.

TIP

Liqueurs such as Grand Marnier, amaretto and limoncello can also be added to enhance the syrup's flavour.

Flavourings

Vanilla Add 1 teaspoon good-quality vanilla extract
Lemon Replace the water with freshly squeezed, finely strained lemon juice
Orange Replace the water with freshly squeezed, finely strained orange juice

Cake portion guide

The following guide indicates about how many portions you get from the different sizes of cake.
The number of portions are based on them being about 2.5cm (1in) square and 9cm (3½in) deep.
You may choose to allow smaller portions for fruit cake, as it's a lot richer.

Size	10cm (4in)		13cm (5in)		15cm (6in)		18cm (7in)		20cm (8in)		23cm (9in)		25cm (10in)		28cm (11in)	
Shape	o	sq	o	sq	o	sq	o	sq	o	sq	o	sq	o	sq	o	sq
Portions	5	10	10	15	20	25	30	40	40	50	50	65	65	85	85	100

Filling and covering quantities

The chart below will give you a guide to how much buttercream or ganache you need to layer
and cover different-sized cakes and cupcakes (see Buttercream and Ganache).

Size	10cm (4in)	13cm (5in) 10–12 cupcakes	15cm (6in)	18cm (7in)	20cm (8in)	23cm (9in)	25cm (10in)	28cm (11in)
Buttercream or ganache	175g (6oz)	250g (9oz)	350g (12oz)	500g (1lb 2oz)	650g (1lb 7oz)	800g (1lb 12oz)	1.1kg (2lb 8oz)	1.25kg (2lb 12oz)

BAKING & COVERING TECHNIQUES

PREPARING CAKE TINS

Before baking, you need to line the bottom and sides of the cake tin to prevent your cake from sticking.

1 Grease the inside of the tin with a little melted butter or sunflower oil spray first to help the paper stick and sit securely in the tin without curling up.

2 For round cakes, to line the bottom, lay your tin on a piece of greaseproof (wax) paper or baking parchment and draw around it using an edible pen. Cut on the inside of the line so that the circle is a good fit inside the tin. Put to one side. Cut a long strip of greaseproof (wax) paper or baking parchment at least 9cm (3½in) wide, fold over one of the long sides about 1cm (3/8in) and crease firmly, then open out. Cut slits from the edge nearest to the fold up to the fold 2.5cm (1in) apart. Put the strip around the inside of tin, with the fold tucked into the bottom corner, then add the base circle and smooth down.

3 For square cakes, lay a piece of greaseproof (wax) paper or baking parchment over the top of the tin. Cut a square that overlaps it on each side by 7.5cm (3in). Cut a slit at each end on two opposite sides. Push the paper inside the tin and fold in the flaps.

LAYERING, FILLING AND PREPARATION

Preparing a cake for icing is one of the key processes in achieving a smooth and perfectly shaped cake. Sponge cakes usually consist of two or three layers (see Classic Sponge Cake), but fruit cakes are kept whole (see Traditional Fruit Cake).

MATERIALS	EQUIPMENT
❖ Buttercream or ganache (see Buttercream and Ganache), for filling and covering	❖ Cake leveller
	❖ Large serrated knife
	❖ Ruler
	❖ Small, sharp paring knife (optional)
❖ Sugar syrup (see Sugar Syrup), for brushing	❖ Cake board, plus chopping board or large cake board if needed
❖ Jam or conserve (jelly or preserves), for filling (optional)	❖ Turntable
	❖ Palette knives
	❖ Pastry brush

1 Cut the dark-baked crust from the base of your cakes. If you have two sponges of equal depths, use a cake leveller to cut them to the same height. If you have baked one-third of your cake mixture in one tin and two-thirds in the other, cut two layers from the deeper sponge with a large serrated knife or cake leveller so that you end up with three layers. Alternatively, you can cut three layers from a larger square cake, piecing together the third layer, as shown opposite. Your finished, prepared cake will be on a 1.25cm (½in) cake board, so the height of your sponge layers together should be about 9cm (3½in) deep.

2 You should have either baked your cake 2.5cm (1in) larger all round than required or baked a larger sponge (see Classic Sponge Cake). Cut around your cake board (this will be the size of your cake), cutting straight down without angling the knife inwards or outwards. For round cakes, use a small, sharp paring knife to do this and for square cakes use a large serrated one.

3 Once you have cut three layers of sponge, put them together to check that they are all even and level, trimming away any sponge if necessary. Place your base cake board on a turntable. If the board is smaller than the turntable, put a chopping board or another large cake board underneath. Use a non-slip mat if necessary.

4 Using a medium-sized palette knife, spread a small amount of buttercream or ganache onto the cake board and stick down your bottom layer of sponge. Brush sugar syrup over the cake – how much will depend on how moist you would like your cake to be.

5 Evenly spread a layer of buttercream or ganache about 3mm (⅛in) thick over the sponge, then a thin layer of jam or conserve (jelly or preserves) if you are using any.

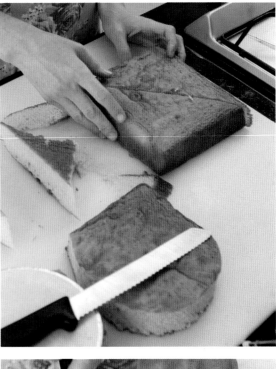

6 Repeat this procedure for the next layer. Finish by adding the top layer and brushing with more sugar syrup.

TIP

Be careful not to add too much filling or it will sink when the icing goes on and ridges in the cake will appear.

7 Cover the sides of the cake in buttercream or ganache, then the top – you only need a very thin and even layer. If the coating becomes 'grainy' as it picks up crumbs from the cake, put it in the refrigerator to set for about 15 minutes and go over it again with a thin second coat. This undercoat is referred to as a 'crumb coat' and is often necessary for carved and sculpted cakes (see below), helping to seal the sponge.

8 Refrigerate your prepared cake for at least 1 hour so that it is firm before attempting to cover it with icing or marzipan; larger cakes will need a little longer.

CARVING AND SCULPTING CAKES

It is much easier to carve and sculpt cakes when they are very firm or almost frozen, so chill, wrapped in clingfilm (plastic wrap), in the freezer beforehand. This technique is used for the Masquerade cake, and specific instructions are given with this project (see Venetian Masquerade). When you come to carve or sculpt your cake, cut the sponge away little by little to prevent removing too much, especially if you are a beginner. Once you have achieved the desired shape, cover the cake with buttercream, or ganache if it's a chocolate cake, filling in any holes as you go (see above). Refrigerate until set and firm enough to cover with icing.

COVERING WITH MARZIPAN AND SUGARPASTE

Make sure that your cake is smoothly covered with buttercream or ganache before you ice it (see above), because if there are any irregularities or imperfections left, you will see them through the icing. You can cover cakes with a second coat of icing if necessary, or cover your cake with a layer of marzipan before you ice it with sugarpaste.

MATERIALS

❖ Marzipan (optional)

❖ Sugarpaste

❖ Icing (confectioners') sugar, for
   dusting (optional)

EQUIPMENT

❖ Greaseproof (wax) paper
   or baking parchment

❖ Scissors

❖ Large non-stick rolling pin

❖ Large non-stick board with
   non-slip mat (optional)

❖ Icing and marzipan spacers

❖ Needle scriber

❖ Icing smoother

❖ Small sharp knife

Round cakes

1 Cut a piece of greaseproof (wax) paper or baking parchment about 7.5cm (3in) larger all round than your cake and put the cake on top.

2 Knead your marzipan or sugarpaste until it is soft. Roll it out with a large non-stick rolling pin on a large non-stick board, which usually won't need dusting with icing (confectioners' sugar), set over a non-stick mat. Otherwise, just use a work surface dusted with icing (confectioners') sugar. Use the spacers to give you the correct width – about 5mm ($^3/_{16}$in). Lift the sugarpaste up with the rolling pin to release from the board and turn it a quarter turn before laying it back down to roll again. Try to keep it a round shape so that it will fit over your cake easily.

3 Pick the sugarpaste up on your rolling pin and lay it over your cake. Quickly but carefully use your hands to smooth it around and down the side of the cake. Pull the sugarpaste away from the side of the cake as you go until you reach the base. Try to push out any air bubbles that may occur or use a needle scriber to burst them carefully.

4 When the icing is on, use a smoother in a circular motion to go over the top of the cake. For the side of the cake, go around in forward circular movements, almost cutting the excess paste at the base. Trim the excess with a small sharp knife and use the smoother to go round the cake one final time to make sure that it is perfectly smooth.

Square cakes

Square cakes are iced in a similar way to round cakes, but pay attention to the corners to ensure that the icing doesn't tear. Use your hands to carefully cup the icing around the corners before you start working it down the sides. Mend any tears with clean soft icing as soon as possible so that the icing blends together well.

TIP

You need to work quite quickly with icing, as it will soon start to dry out and crack. Keep any leftover icing well wrapped in a plastic bag to prevent it from drying out.

ICING CAKE BOARDS

Covering the base cake board with icing makes a huge difference to the finished cake, giving it a clean, professional finish. By carefully choosing the right colour for the icing, the board can be incorporated into the design of the cake itself.

Moisten the board with some water. Roll out the sugarpaste to 4mm (a generous ⅛in), ideally using icing or marzipan spacers. Pick the icing up on the rolling pin and lay it over the cake board. Place the board either on a turntable or bring it towards the edge of the work surface so that the icing is hanging down over it. Use your icing smoother in a downwards motion to cut a smooth edge around the board. Cut away any excess. Finish by smoothing the top using circular movements to achieve a flat and perfectly smooth surface for your cake to sit on. Leave to dry overnight.

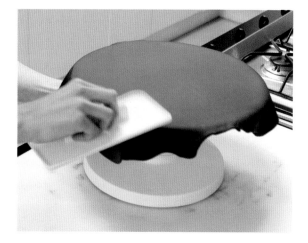

Marzipan and sugarpaste quantities

This following charts give an estimate of the quantities you will need to cover different-sized cakes and cake boards; square cakes will require slightly more than round cakes. If you are not very experienced at covering cakes, allow a bit extra than specified here. These quantities are based on cakes about 9cm (3½in) deep.

COVERING CAKES

Cake size	15cm (6in)	18cm (7in)	20cm (8in)	23cm (9in)	25cm (10in)	28cm (11in)	30cm (12in)
Covering cake (marzipan/ sugarpaste)	650g (1lb 2oz)	750g (1lb 7oz)	850g (1lb 10oz)	1kg (1lb 14oz)	1.25kg (2lb 12oz)	1.5kg (3lb 5oz)	1.75kg (3lb 13oz)

COVERING CAKE BOARDS

Cake board size	23cm (9in)	25cm (10in)	28cm (11in)	30cm (12in)	33cm (13in)	35cm (14in)
Icing cake board	600g (1lb 5oz)	650g (1lb 7oz)	725g (1lb 9½oz)	850g (1lb 14oz)	1kg (2lb 4oz)	1.2kg (2lb 10oz)

SECURING RIBBON AROUND CAKE BOARDS

To finish your cake off in style, attach some double-faced satin ribbon around the board to coordinate with the cake design and colour scheme. I use 1.5cm (⅝in) -wide ribbon for this. Stick the ribbon in place with double-sided tape at intervals around the board.

┌─ TIP ─────────────────────────
  For square cakes, put the double-sided tape
  around each corner, as well as a small piece
  in the centre of each side.
└───────────────────────────────

ASSEMBLING TIERED CAKES

Stacking cakes on top of one another is not a difficult process, but it needs to be done in the right way so that you can rest assured that the cake is structurally sound. I prefer to use hollow plastic dowels, as they are very sturdy and easily cut to the correct height. Thinner plastic dowels can be used for smaller cakes. As a general guide, use three dowels for a round cake and four for square. Use more dowels for larger cakes.

MATERIALS

❖ Stiff royal icing (see Royal Icing)

❖ Iced cake board (see Icing Cake Boards)

110 *Baking and Covering Techniques*

EQUIPMENT

+ Cake-top marking template
+ Needle scriber or marking tool
+ Hollow plastic dowels
+ Edible pen
+ Large serrated knife
+ Spare cake board
+ Spirit level
+ Icing smoothers

1 Use the cake-top marking template to find the centre of your base cake.

2 Using a needle scriber or marking tool, mark the cake where the dowels should go. These need to be positioned well inside the diameter of the cake to be stacked on top.

3 Push a dowel into the cake where it has been marked. Using an edible pen, mark the dowel where it meets the top of the cake.

TIP

If your cake is slightly uneven, push the dowel into the tallest part of the cake.

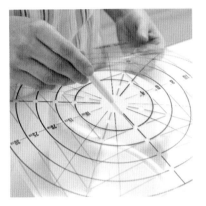

4 Remove the dowel and cut it at the mark with a serrated knife. Cut the other dowels to the same height and insert them all into the cake. Place a cake board on top of the dowels and check that they are equal in height by using a spirit level on the board.

5 Stick your base cake onto the centre of your iced cake board with some stiff royal icing. Use your smoothers to move it into position if necessary. Allow the icing to set for a few minutes before stacking on the next tier. Repeat to attach a third tier, if using.

TIP

Wait a couple of minutes before moving the assembled cakes so that the icing has had time to set a little.

MINIATURE CAKES

These cakes are cut from larger pieces of cake (see Basic Cake Recipes) and are layered, filled and iced
in a similar fashion to the larger cakes. Bake a square cake and cut your cakes from this, either round
or square. The size of the cake will depend on how many cakes you require and the size you would like
them to be. Always choose a slightly larger size of cake than you need to allow for wastage. For nine
5cm (2in) square mini cakes (I usually make them this size), you would need an 18cm (7in) square cake.
Use only two-thirds of the quantities of ingredients in the charts, as mini cakes are not as deep as large
cakes. Bake all the mixture in one tin rather than dividing it between two for larger cakes.

MATERIALS

❖ Large square baked
   classic sponge cake
   or classic chocolate
   cake (see Basic
   Cake Recipes)
❖ Sugar syrup (see
   Sugar Syrup)
❖ Buttercream or
   ganache (see
   Buttercream and
   Ganache)
❖ Sugarpaste
❖

EQUIPMENT

❖ Cake leveller
❖ Circle cutter or
   serrated knife
❖ Pastry brush
❖ Cake card (optional)
❖ Palette knife
❖ Large non-stick
   rolling pin
❖ Large non-stick
   board with non-slip
   mat
❖ Metal ruler
❖ Large sharp knife
❖ Large circle cutter
   or small sharp knife
❖ 2 icing smoothers

---TIP---

For mini traditional fruit cakes, bake the
mixture in small, individual tins, as they can't
be cut out due to the structure of the cakes.

---TIP---

It's much easier to work with the sponge if
it's very cold, as it will be a good deal firmer.

1 Slice your large square cake horizontally into
two even layers using a cake leveller. Cut small
individual rounds (using a cutter) or squares (using
a serrated knife).

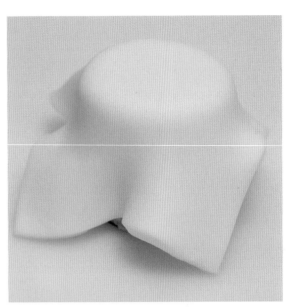

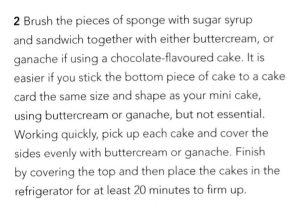

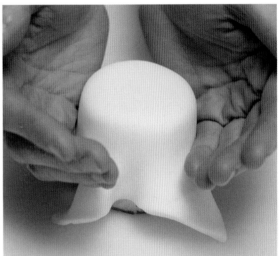

2 Brush the pieces of sponge with sugar syrup and sandwich together with either buttercream, or ganache if using a chocolate-flavoured cake. It is easier if you stick the bottom piece of cake to a cake card the same size and shape as your mini cake, using buttercream or ganache, but not essential. Working quickly, pick up each cake and cover the sides evenly with buttercream or ganache. Finish by covering the top and then place the cakes in the refrigerator for at least 20 minutes to firm up.

3 Roll out a piece of sugarpaste 38cm (15in) square and 5mm (³/₁₆in) thick with a large non-stick rolling pin on a large non-stick board set over a non-slip mat. Cut nine small squares and lay one over each cake. If you are a beginner, do half the cakes at a time, keeping the other squares under clingfilm (plastic wrap) to prevent them drying out.

4 Use your hands to work the icing down around the sides of the cake and trim away the excess with a large circle cutter or small sharp knife.

5 Use two icing smoothers on either side of the cake going forwards and backwards and turning the cake as you go to create a perfectly smooth result. Leave the icing to dry, ideally overnight, before decorating the cakes.

BAKING CUPCAKES

Cupcakes are made in exactly the same way as
the classic sponge cake, classic chocolate cake or
carrot cake (see Basic Cake Recipes). The amount of
ingredients you need will depend on the size of your
cases. For 10–12 cupcakes, use the quantities given
for a 13cm (5in) round or 10cm (4in) square cake. Use
cupcakes cases (liners) to bake the mixture, placing
them in tartlet tins or muffin trays and filling two-
thirds to three-quarters full. Bake in a preheated oven
at 180°C/350°F/Gas Mark 4 for about 20 minutes until
springy to the touch.

Cupcake cases (liners) come in plain or patterned
paper, or in foil in a range of colours. I prefer to use
plain foil ones, as they keep the cakes fresh and don't
detract from the decoration on the cakes. But you
can use decorative cases (liners) for plainer cupcakes.

Cupcakes can be iced in various ways, depending on
the look and taste you want to achieve. While some
techniques are more involved and a little tricky to
accomplish, others are much simpler and are a great
way to get the children involved.

DECORATING CUPCAKES WITH BUTTERCREAM

This is the simplest way to decorate cupcakes. You
can pipe the buttercream on using a large plastic
piping (pastry) bag fitted with either a plain or star-
shaped tube (tip), which will take a little practice to
get each cake looking perfect. Alternatively, simply
use a palette knife to spread the buttercream on
evenly to create an attractive domed top.

TIP

You may need to re-beat your buttercream
to ensure that it's soft when you use it.

FONDANT-DIPPED CUPCAKES

This way of decorating cupcakes is much more involved, but liquid fondant really makes a delicious and lovely looking little cake. I have used ready-made fondant here, which you can buy from specialist suppliers, but you can use a powdered fondant instead, available from most good supermarkets.

1 Shave off any uneven bumps with a small, sharp serrated knife so that the cakes are perfectly shaped. Brush the tops with the flavoured sugar syrup.

2 Bring the apricot masking spread or strained jam (jelly) to the boil in a saucepan and leave to cool slightly before brushing over the cupcakes with a pastry brush. Refrigerate for at least 15–30 minutes.

3 Put the fondant in a microwave-proof bowl and warm in the microwave for about 1½ minutes on medium power until it can be easily poured.

4 Add the glucose and three-quarters of the unflavoured sugar syrup and gently stir together, trying to avoid introducing too many air bubbles. Add any colouring. If you are dipping cakes in more than one colour, split the fondant between two or more bowls beforehand. Cover the bowl or bowls you are not using immediately with clingfilm (plastic wrap).

MATERIALS (MAKES 20)

* 20 domed-shaped cupcakes (see opposite)
* 1 quantity sugar syrup, flavoured to match the sponge, and 1 quantity unflavoured (see Sugar Syrup)
* 100g (3½oz) apricot masking spread or strained jam (jelly)
* 1kg (2lb 4oz) tub ready-made fondant
* 1 tablespoon liquid glucose
* Food colouring, as required

EQUIPMENT

* Small, sharp serrated knife
* Pastry brush
* Microwave oven and microwave-proof bowl
* 2 metal spoons or palette knife

5 Return the fondant to the microwave and heat it gently until slightly warmer than body temperature (39–40°C/102–104°F). Test the consistency by dipping one of the cupcakes into the fondant. If it is too thick, add the remaining unflavoured sugar syrup until the fondant coats the cupcake well. Be careful not make it too runny or the fondant won't set.

6 Dip the tops of the cupcakes one at a time in the fondant, holding the cake by its case (liner). Allow the excess to drip down for a second and turn it back up the right way to set. Once you have dipped all the cupcakes, you may need to give them a second coating; wait 5–10 minutes for the first coat to dry.

FONDANT FANCIES

These are a great alternative to cupcakes. Like the mini cakes (see Miniature Cakes), they are cut from a square or rectangular classic sponge cake (see Classic Sponge Cake) and can be a variety of shapes, although the easiest to make are square. If they are to fit in a cupcake case (liner), they should be about 4cm (1½in) square and 4cm (1½in) high. Bake shallow cakes (see Materials right) and trim the top and bottom to give you the correct height. Vanilla, lemon or orange-flavoured sponge works best for fondant fancies.

The fondant icing is prepared in the same way as for the cupcakes (see Baking Cupcakes), but the technique used when dipping them is quite different.

1 Once you have layered, filled and stuck the sponge back together, brush the remaining flavoured sugar syrup over the top of the sponge before covering it with a thin layer of the apricot masking spread or jam (jelly).

MATERIALS (MAKES 16)

❖ 18cm (7in) square shallow classic sponge cake (see Classic Sponge Cake, but use half the quantities specified), split into two layers and filled with jam (jelly), marmalade or lemon, lime or orange curd (see Layering, Filling and Preparation)

❖ 1 quantity sugar syrup, flavoured to match the sponge, and 1 quantity unflavoured (see Sugar Syrup)

❖ 2 tablespoons apricot masking spread or strained jam (jelly), boiled and slightly cooled

❖ 175g (6oz) marzipan or sugarpaste

❖ 750g (1lb 10oz) ready-made fondant

❖ ¾ tablespoon liquid glucose

❖ Food colouring, as required

EQUIPMENT

❖ Pastry brush
❖ Large non-stick rolling pin
❖ Large non-stick board with non-slip mat
❖ Icing or marzipan spacers
❖ Icing smoothers
❖ Metal ruler
❖ Large and small sharp knife
❖ Dipping fork
❖ Wire rack
❖ 16 cupcake cases (liners)

2 Roll the marzipan or sugarpaste out with a large non-stick rolling pin on a large non-stick board set over a non-slip mat to 3–4mm (1/8in) thick, using the spacers to guide you. Lay it over your sponge and run the smoother over the top so that it is firmly stuck down. Mark and cut 4cm (1½in) squares with a sharp knife, keeping the squares together until you are ready to dip them. Place the sponge in the refrigerator and chill for at least 1 hour.

3 Prepare the fondant by following Steps 3–5 for Fondant-dipped Cupcakes, using the unflavoured sugar syrup.

4 Cut away any excess trimmings from the sponge. Plunge each square fancy, marzipan/icing side down, into your warm fondant. Working quickly, use the dipping fork to turn the fancy back upwards and move it across to the wire rack to allow the excess icing to drip down and off the sides of the cake. Repeat for each fancy.

5 Remove the fancies from the rack using a small sharp knife to cut away any excess fondant.

6 Place each fancy into a cupcake case (liner) that has been slightly pressed out beforehand so that the cake fits easily inside. Cup the case (liner) back up around the sides of the cake so that it takes on its shape. Place the fancies together, side by side, until they are completely set and ready to decorate.

BAKING COOKIES

Cookies are great fun to make – ideal for getting children involved – and are suitable for just about any occasion. You can cut out any shapes from the cookie dough and decorate them however you like. In this book, you will learn how to use a variety of techniques to create eye-catching and delicious treats that are sure to impress.

MATERIALS (MAKES 10–15 LARGE OR 25–30 MEDIUM)

- ❖ 250g (9oz) unsalted butter
- ❖ 250g (9oz) caster (superfine) sugar
- ❖ 1–2 medium eggs
- ❖ 1 teaspoon vanilla extract
- ❖ 500g (1lb 2oz) plain (all-purpose) flour, plus extra for dusting

EQUIPMENT

- ❖ Large electric mixer
- ❖ Spatula
- ❖ Deep tray or plastic container
- ❖ Clingfilm (plastic wrap)
- ❖ Rolling pin
- ❖ Cookie cutters or templates
- ❖ Sharp knife (if using templates)
- ❖ Baking trays
- ❖ Greaseproof (wax) paper or baking parchment

TIP

The cookie dough can be made up to two weeks ahead or stored in the freezer until ready to use.

1 In a bowl of an electric mixer, beat the butter and sugar together until creamy and quite fluffy.

2 Add the eggs and vanilla extract and mix until they are well combined.

3 Sift the flour, add to the bowl and mix until all the ingredients just come together. You may need to do this in two stages – do not over-mix.

4 Tip the dough into a container lined with clingfilm (plastic wrap) and press down firmly. Cover with clingfilm (plastic wrap) and refrigerate for at least 30 minutes.

5 On a work surface lightly dusted with flour, roll out the cookie dough to about 4mm (1/8in) thick. Sprinkle a little extra flour on top of the dough as you roll to prevent it from sticking to the rolling pin.

TIP

Be careful not too add too much flour when you are rolling out your dough, as it will become too dry.

6 Cut out your shapes either with cutters or using templates and a sharp knife. Place on baking trays lined with greaseproof (wax) paper or baking parchment and return to the refrigerator to rest for at least 30 minutes.

7 Bake the cookies in a preheated oven at 180°C/350°F/Gas Mark 4 for about 10 minutes, depending on their size, or until they are golden brown. Leave them to cool completely before storing them in an airtight container until you are ready to decorate them. The baked cookies will keep for up to one month.

Flavour variations

Chocolate Substitute 50g (1¾oz) flour with cocoa powder (unsweetened cocoa).
Citrus Add the finely grated zest of 1 lemon or orange.
Almond Replace the vanilla extract with 1 teaspoon almond extract.

DECORATING TECHNIQUES

ROYAL ICING

Working with royal icing is one of the most useful skills to learn in cake decorating. It is a highly versatile medium, as it can be used for icing cakes and cookies, for intricate piping of decorations (borders, flowers and lettering) or for simply attaching and sticking.

The icing is best used as fresh as possible, but it will keep for up to five days in an airtight container. Re-beat the mixture back to its correct consistency before use if it is not used immediately.

1 If using dried egg powder, soak the powder in the water for at least 30 minutes in advance, but ideally overnight in the refrigerator.

2 Sift the icing (confectioners') sugar into the mixing bowl of an electric mixer and add the egg whites or strained reconstituted egg mixture.

3 Mix together on a low speed for about 3–4 minutes until the icing has reached a stiff-peak consistency, which is what you need for sticking on decorations and gluing cakes together.

MATERIALS

✤ 2 medium egg whites or 15g (½oz) dried egg albumen powder mixed with 75ml (2½fl oz) water

✤ 500g (1lb 2oz) icing (confectioners') sugar

EQUIPMENT

✤ Large electric mixer
✤ Sieve (strainer)
✤ Spatula

4 Store the icing in an airtight container covered with a damp, clean cloth to prevent it from drying out.

Soft-peak royal icing

In order to pipe various patterns and decorations easily, you may need to add a tiny amount of water to your royal icing so that the consistency is a bit softer.

'RUN-OUT' ICING

Royal icing is thinned down with more water to 'flood' (fill in) cookies (see opposite). For the desired consistency, test the icing by lifting your spoon and letting the icing drip back into the bowl. The icing falling back into the bowl should remain on the surface for five seconds before disappearing. If it is too runny it will run over the outlines and sides of the cookies, but if it is too stiff it won't spread very well.

ROYAL-ICED COOKIES

This is my favourite method of icing cookies, as I love the taste of the crisp white icing against the softer texture of the cookie underneath. Most of the cookie projects in this book have been iced this way. If you are icing a large quantity of cookies, use a squeezable plastic bottle with a small tube instead of piping (pastry) bags.

MATERIALS
❖ Soft-peak royal icing (see opposite)

EQUIPMENT
❖ Paper piping (pastry) bags, small and large (see Making a Piping/Pastry Bag)
❖ Piping tubes (tips): nos. 1 and 1.5 or 2

TIP

If the area you need to 'flood' is relatively large, work round the edges of the piped outline and then work inwards to the centre to ensure an even covering.

1 Place the no. 1.5 or 2 tube (tip) in a small piping (pastry) bag and fill with some soft-peak royal icing. Pipe an outline around the edge of each cookie.

2 Thin down some more royal icing with water until 'flooding' consistency (see Royal Icing) and place in a large piping (pastry) bag fitted with the no. 1 tube. Use to flood inside the outlines on the cookies with icing. For larger cookies or 'run-outs' (see 'Run-out Icing), you can snip off the tip of the bag instead of using a tube (tip).

3 Once dry, pipe over any details that are required and stick on any decorations.

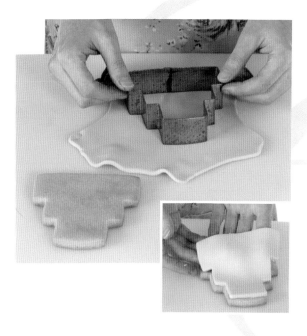

COVERING COOKIES WITH SUGARPASTE

This is a very simple and quick way to ice cookies, yet still looks really neat and effective. Roll out some sugarpaste to no more than 4mm (1/8in) thick and cut out the shape of the cookie using the same cutter or template used for the cookie dough. Stick the icing onto the cookie using boiled and cooled apricot masking spread or strained jam (jelly), taking care not to stretch it out of shape.

MAKING A PIPING (PASTRY) BAG

1 Cut two equal triangles from a large square of greaseproof (wax) paper or baking parchment. As a guide, for small bags cut from a 15–20cm (6–8in) square and for large bags cut from a 30–35cm (12–14in) square.

2 Keeping the centre point towards you with the longest side furthest away, curl the right-hand corner inwards and bring the point to meet the centre point. Adjust your hold so that you have the two points together between your right thumb and index finger.

3 With your left hand, curl the left point inwards, bringing it across the front and around to the back of the other two points in the centre of the cone. Adjust your grip again so that you are now holding the three points together with both thumbs and index fingers.

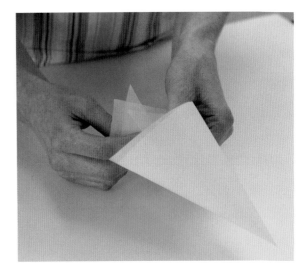

4 Tighten the cone-shaped bag by gently rubbing your thumb and index fingers forwards and backwards until you have a sharp tip at the end of the bag.

5 Carefully fold the back of the bag (where all the points meet) inwards, making sure that you press hard along the fold. Repeat this to ensure that it is really secure.

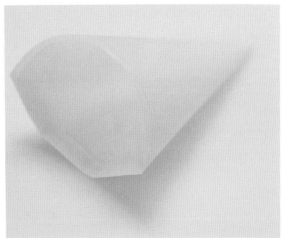

TIP

Make lots of piping (pastry) bags at a time and put them aside for a decorating session.

PIPING WITH ROYAL ICING

For basic piping work, use soft-peak royal icing (see Royal Icing). The size of the tube (tip) you use will depend on the job at hand and how competent you are.

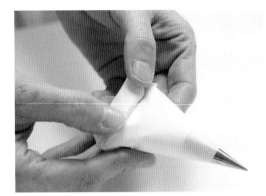

Fill the piping (pastry) bag until it is no more than one-third full. Fold the top over, away from the join, until you have a tight and well-sealed bag. The correct way to hold the piping (pastry) bag is important. Use your index finger to guide the bag. You can also use your other hand to guide you if it's easier.

To pipe dots, squeeze the icing out gently until you have the dot that's the size you want. Stop squeezing, then lift the bag. If there is a peak in the icing, use a damp brush to flatten it down.

To pipe teardrops, once you have squeezed out the dot, pull the tube (tip) through the dot, then release the pressure and lift the bag (see Elegant Mini Cakes).

To pipes lines, touch the tube (tip) down, then lift the bag up in a smooth movement, squeezing gently. Decrease the pressure and touch it back down to the point where you want the line to finish. Try not to drag the icing along, or it will become uneven. Use a template or a cookie outline as a guide where possible.

To pipe a 'snail trail' border, squeeze out a large dot of icing and drag the tube (tip) through it to one side like a teardrop. Repeat this motion around the cake.

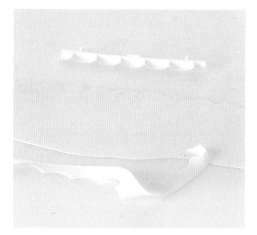

WORKING WITH FLOWER PASTE

Flower paste is used for creating more delicate decorations for cakes and cookies, such as flowers, frills, bows and streamers, as it can be rolled out really thinly. Before using, knead the paste well by continuously pulling it apart with your fingers.

MODELLING PASTE AND CMC

Modelling paste is basically a stiffer version of sugarpaste, which enables you to mould larger, less delicate shapes and objects. It isn't as strong and won't dry out as quickly as flower paste. You can buy ready-made modelling paste, but it is really simple and cheaper to make your own using CMC (sodium carboxymethyl cellulose). This comes in the form of a powder, which you knead into the sugarpaste; use about 1 teaspoon per 300g (10½oz) icing.

TIP

Always add your colouring gradually and keep some extra white icing to hand in case you make a mistake.

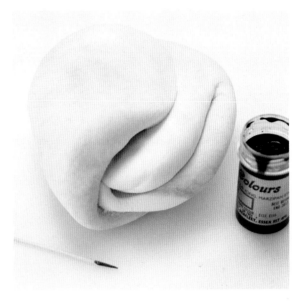

COLOURING ICINGS

There are two types of colouring used to colour icing: paste and liquid. I prefer to use paste colours, especially when colouring sugarpaste, flower paste and marzipan, to prevent the icing from becoming too wet and sticky. Small amounts can be added with a cocktail stick (toothpick) and larger amounts with a knife, then kneaded into the icing. Liquid colours work well with royal icing and liquid fondant, but be careful not to add too much too soon.

Be aware that the colour of your icing can often change as it dries. Some colours tend to fade, while others darken.

TIP

It's always advisable to colour more icing than you need to allow for any mishaps, and quantities given in the recipes are generous. Any leftovers can be stored in an airtight bag in a sealed container for future use.

TEMPLATES

(All shown at actual size)
Lacy Lovely/Irresistible Ivory
Cake – floral and leaf templates

Venetian Masquerade
– large mask

Masked Beauty Cupcakes
– small masks

Eastern Shoe Cookies
– shoe

Beautiful
Bunting
– bunting
triangles

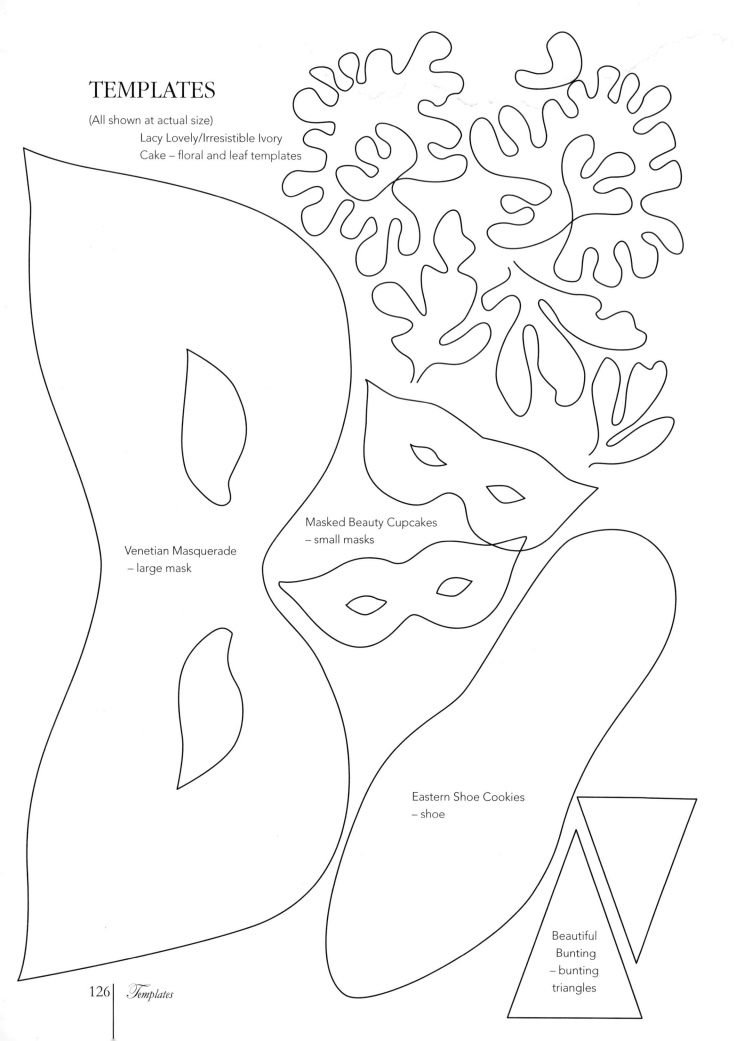

SUPPLIERS

UK

Cakes for Fun
www.cakes4fun.co.uk
100 Lower Richmond Road,
London, SW15 1LN
Tel: 020 8785 9039

The Cake Parlour
www.thecakeparlour.com
146 Arthur Road, London,
SW19 8AQ
Tel: 020 8947 4424

Cox & Cox
www.coxandcox.co.uk
Marshall Way, Commerce Park,
Frome, Somerset, BA11 2FB
Tel: 0844 858 0734

FMM Sugarcraft
www.fmmsugarcraft.com
Unit 7, Chancerygate Business
Park, Whiteleaf Road, Hemel
Hempstead, Herts, HP3 9HD
Tel: 01442 292970

Lindy's Cakes Ltd
www.lindyscakes.co.uk
Unit 2, Station Approach,
Wendover, Aylesbury,
Buckinghamshire, HP22 6BN
Tel: 01296 622418

Orchard Products
www.orchardproducts.co.uk
51 Hallyburton Road, Hove,
East Sussex, BN3 7GP
Tel: 01273 419418

Squire's Kitchen Shop
www.squires-shop.com
3 Waverley Lane, Farnham,
Surrey, GU9 8BB
Tel: 0845 225 5671

Sugarshack
www.sugarshack.co.uk
Unit 12, Bowmans Trading Estate,
Westmoreland Road,
London, NW9 9RL
Tel: 020 8204 2994

Sunflower SugarArt
www.sunflower-sugarart.co.uk
Tel: 01427 874890

Surbiton Sugar Art
www.surbitonart.co.uk
140 Hook Road, Surbiton,
London, KT6 5BZ
Tel: 0845 260 1945

US

Designer Stencils
www.designerstencils.com
Designer Stencils, 2503 Silverside
Road, Wilmington, DE 19810
Tel: 800-822-7836

Global Sugar Art
www.globalsugarart.com
625 Route 3, Unit 3, Plattsburgh,
New York 12901
Tel: 1-518-561-3039

ACKNOWLEDGMENTS

After the fun and fabulous feedback I received from my first two books, I couldn't wait to produce another and I'd like to thank everyone who has made this possible. Many thanks again to David & Charles, in particular Jeni Hennah, Kevin Mansfield and Sarah Underhill, and my editor Bethany Dymond, proof-reader Jo Richardson and photographer Sian Irvine – it has been a pleasure working with you once more.

Thanks to all the suppliers who kindly sent such wonderful products to complement the cakes and cookies: The Crockery Cupboard (www.thecrockerycupboard.co.uk) for the delightful colourful crockery, Zita Elze (www.zitaelze.com) for the beautiful flowers, Lisbeth Dahl (www.lisbethdahl.com) for the gorgeous trinket boxes, glass stands and snowflake decorations, Maroque (www.maroque.co.uk) for all the fabulous items featured in the Arabian Nights projects, Tanya Whelan (www. grandrevivaldesign.com) for providing the pretty prints for the bunting cake and Farrow and Ball (www.farrow-ball.com) for the Toile Trellis (Sweet Sunshine), Drag (Arabian Nights) and Brockhampton Star (Winter Wonderland) wallpapers.

A big thank you goes to my two friends and colleagues Holly and Beth for all their help and suggestions, and finally, huge thanks to my wonderful and supportive husband and family for the their patience and encouragement as always.

ABOUT THE AUTHOR

After being inspired by making her own wedding cake in 2005, Zoe turned passion into profession and headed to London to work with some of the most prestigious bakers in the business. Along the way she developed her unique style and skills, and subsequently set up her own business in 2008. Zoe's cake creations have drawn attention from both clients and the press, and she was awarded *Perfect Wedding*'s 'Best Wedding Cake Designer 2010' award. Zoe has previously published two titles for D&C. Following her success, Zoe has opened a new boutique in Wimbledon called The Cake Parlour.

INDEX